SECOND • EDITION

SERVING
—*AND*—
SURVIVING
As a Human-Service Worker

SECOND · EDITION

SERVING
— AND —
SURVIVING
As a Human-Service Worker

J. ROBERT RUSSO
Southern Illinois University

WAVELAND
PRESS, INC.
Prospect Heights, Illinois

For information about this book, write or call:

Waveland Press, Inc.
P.O. Box 400
Prospect Heights, Illinois 60070
(708) 634-0081

Cover Design: Miriam Recio

ISBN 0-88133-691-2

Printed in the United States of America

7   6   5   4   3   2   1

Contents

Preface to the Second Edition **ix**

Chapter 1 Introduction 1

Job Selection, Application, and Interview   1
   Initial Choices   2
   Sources of Job-Related Information   2
   Job Applications   3
   The Interview   4
   The First Three Months   5
The Organization's Norms   6
   Conflict Between You and the Norms   7
   Feedback   11
   Adjustment to Failure   13
Summary   13
Discussion Questions   14
References   14

Chapter 2 The People 15

Clients   15
Your Feelings About Clients   20
   Dealing with Clients   21
Staff Members   23
The Urge to Change the Organization   26
The Important People   30
   Clients' Rights   30
   Former Clients as Staff Members   32
Summary   33
Discussion Questions   33
References   34

Chapter 3   The Organization   35

The Board   37
Some Administrative Types   39
The Boss's Job   43
   Assistants   44
   Your Immediate Supervisor   44
Organizational Control   47
Organizational Reorganization   48
The Shadow Organization   50
Summary   52
Discussion Questions   53
References   53

Chapter 4   Your Coworkers   55

Patterns of Adjustment   57
   Identifying with Clients   58
   Identifying with Coworkers   59
   Identifying with the Organization   60
Staff Meetings   61
Traditional Staff Categories   64
   Nonprofessional   64
   Paraprofessional   64
   Professional   65
   Communication Between Categories   66
Socialization   70
   Socialization of Social Workers   71
   The Socialization of Teachers   72
   The Socialization of Nurses   74
   The Socialization of Police Officers   75
Socialization in Human-Service Occupations   76
Volunteer Staff Members   77
   The Growth of the Volunteer Movement   77
   Pros and Cons   78
Conclusion   80
Summary   81
Discussion Questions   81
References   82

Chapter 5   Community Based Programs   85

Historical Context   85
Deinstitutionalization   86
The Mentally Ill   87
   State Mental Hospitals Today   89
   Nursing Homes   90

Community Residential Care   91
Homelessness   92
Outreach Programs   94
Roles for Human-Service Workers   95
Volunteer Boards and Paid Staff   97
Organizational Continuity   98
Summary   98
Discussion Questions   99
References   99

Chapter 6   The Other Establishments 101
Referral   102
Different Agencies; Different Priorities   103
Interorganizational Cooperation   107
Summary   111
Discussion Questions   111
References   111

Chapter 7   Helplessness and Hope 113
Burnout: Its Treatment and Control   117
So You Want to Change the Organization   123
Some Conditions That Facilitate Change   128
Conflict, Competition, and Cooperation   136
Remember, You're a Guest   137
Summary   138
Discussion Questions   138
References   139

Chapter 8   Prevention 141
Kinds of Prevention Programs   144
Infants   145
Children in School   146
Lifelong Prevention   147
Medical Prevention   148
Components of Effective Prevention Programs   149
Summary   152
Discussion Questions   153
References   153

**Chapter 9   Odds and Ends From the Present
and a Look at the Future 155**
Human-Service Organizations   155
Committees   155
Consultants   156

Accrediting, Inspecting, and Evaluating Human-Service
   Organizations   156
In-Service Training   157
Job-Related Sex   158
Sexual Harassment   159
Bureaucratic Celebrations and Sympathy   160
Changes in Staff Members   161
Feelings of Failure   162
Don't Lose Your Keys   163
A Look at the Future   164
Drug Abuse Treatment   165
Temporary Homes   167
Homelessness   168
Public Toward Private   169
Local Community Control   170
Legal Influences and Special Interests   170
The Labor Market   171
Summary   173
References   174

Index   177

Preface to the Second Edition

To have a job that you enjoy and get paid for is exciting. The power of a mute's smile for a speech therapist, a student's flash of insight for a teacher, or a patient's first unaided step for a physical therapist is worth more than the paycheck.

These unique events are powerful intermittent rewards that will help motivate you to continue serving. Balancing these rewards with the pressures, policies, procedures, rules, and regulations that control your teaching and help giving is what this book is about. You who work the longest hours, get the lowest pay, and have the most contact with the client, student, resident, or patient are the intended audience. You are the key staff.

Books are written and courses are offered to administrators and bosses on how to "handle" you and run the organization. This book is intended to help *you* deal with your bosses, coworkers, and the organization that pays you. It has been my observation that much of what is taught in teacher training, nursing school, social work programs, and the education of mental health and criminal justice workers is quite remote from the realities of the job. This book is about the realities of serving as a teacher and a human-service worker. It is about the experiences of those who have recently entered these occupations.

Many help givers begin their careers with an idealistic outlook. Along with a paycheck, they hope to receive other professional and personal rewards. When such rewards don't materialize, feelings of frustration and failure may develop. The prevalence of these feelings among teachers and human-service workers prompted me to write this book. It is my intention to help you put such feelings in a perspective that may make the feelings more productive for both you and the people that you teach and serve. You deliver the service and generate the records that the department, administration, or the board uses to survive. Your survival links the organization to its clients.

Many of the experiences related in this book are my own. I have been a recipient, a ward, a client, a patient, and an occasional learner. I have worked as a gang worker, a settlement house director, a teacher, a counselor, a professor, an administrator, a board member, a consultant, and a janitor. This book consists primarily of an organized collection of real life experiences of a group of relatively new teachers and human-service workers. It will be evident why these new employees wished to remain anonymous. Some related literature and research results are also included.

If you are using this book for a course, I hope that you, your instructor, and the other students in your class disagree, discuss, and debate as a result of what I have written. You may be able to provide examples that are more personal and, therefore, more meaningful than the examples others have supplied for the text. I look forward to your comments which can be sent to me in care of the publisher. Readers and reviewers of the first edition were most helpful, and I thank them for their thoughtful comments.

1 Introduction

All bureaucratic institutions have much in common, although the slang, the students, and the clients may differ. Problems that are minor in one may be major in another. This book focuses on those aspects that are common to all kinds of helping institutions. *Helping* here refers to teaching, counseling, training, educating, guiding, nursing, treating, aiding, serving, and so on. As a helping person, you will try to influence or change another person. You will expect your help to be useful and constructive. The other person will be healthier, happier, wiser, more skilled, better adjusted, or better educated as a result of your work.

Many of the examples in this book were collected from taped interviews of recently hired staff members. Each of these individuals wishes to remain anonymous for reasons that will become clear as you read. The prison guards, ward attendants, teachers, counselors, psychologists, youth supervisors, nurses, and social workers relate experiences that may be of help to you as you begin a career as a teacher or human-service worker. These new staff members don't have all the answers, but their successes, as well as their mistakes, may provide some guidance to you in your career of serving others.

Job Selection, Application, and Interview

Here are a few guidelines on job selection, applications, and interviews. We don't choose a single job from the more than 30,000

1

job titles available; instead, we consider entering many occupations during our lives. We develop conceptions of what certain occupations involve. Our choice of jobs is based on these conceptions and the degree to which our conceptions fit our needs, desires, and talents. It is not surprising that human-service workers value working with people more than those who choose careers in business.

Initial Choices

After we select an occupational area, we choose an organization. We make such a decision at the beginning of our career and again when we consider changing jobs. When a tight job market limits job possibilities, it may not seem as though there is much of a choice; but there is. We choose either to stay where we are or to go someplace else. When a *matchup* occurs between our talent and needs and an organization's requirements and characteristics, we are confronted with a choice. When we make such a choice, we develop a psychological contract. These unwritten contracts are developed in our minds. Expectations about the attractive aspects of a new job always are included. The act of choosing seems to distort our perception.

After we decide to take a new job, we tend to see it as even more attractive than we did at the time we made the choice. Moreover, the other alternatives that we may have been considering look much less attractive once we've made our choice. This process of justifying our choice sets us up. The letdown you may feel soon after taking a new job is at least partly related to this process of self-justification. Self-seduction and letdown seem to be common experiences among individuals beginning new careers (Vroom and Deci, 1971; Wanous, 1975; Sheridan, 1975).

Our need to justify our actions is reinforced by job recruiting and advertising practices; seldom are the less desirable elements of a job spelled out in advertisements. Even when you have heard about the job by word of mouth, each person in the information chain has added to and subtracted from the original information; the description you hear may bear little resemblance to the on-the-job situation. Simply put, you should gather as much information as possible before you make your application and begin to develop your psychological contract.

Sources of Job-Related Information

Where can you obtain job-related information? Often, community college and university instructors are reliable sources of information.

This can be especially true of instructors in professional schools. For example, an assessment of mental-health organizations can sometimes be made with information secured from professionals in private practice. Public agencies such as the United Way, accrediting bodies, licensing bureaus, and community referral services can also be valuable sources of information. Court administrators' offices, public defenders' staffs, and public school counselors might be "interviewed" about a job in mental health.

Obtain as many answers to your questions as you can before you accept a position. I have found it useful to use a secondary source of information; that is, when I've located someone who knows about a particular job, I ask them for the name of another person who might know something about the organization involved and I contact them.

Job Applications

If you decide to apply for a position, get a set of application materials. Some organizations may be willing to send them to you while others may request that you pick them up in person. If you write to the organization, the prospective employer has received the first entry in your personnel file — your letter. If you go in person, you have made your first impression. The set of application materials may range from a one-page locally developed form to a complex array of sheets, computer cards, and foldouts designed to be optically scanned and fed into a data processing system.

In any case, the organization will keep your application. If you are hired, your application will become a part of your personnel file, so make sure that it is neat. If your handwriting is cryptic, you should either print or have your application typed. Whatever you do, don't fill out the application hastily in the personnel office on a rough desk with a leaky ballpoint pen. Take the application home with you. Write your answers on scratch paper, and then transfer them to the application. Ask someone to read the application after you've completed it. Most prospective employers appreciate proper grammar, punctuation, and sentence structure.

A carefully worded cover letter (typewritten) should be attached to your application. Federal and state laws restrict the type of information that a prospective employer can request on a job application. Include relevant additional data about yourself in your letter. Some organizations have such a poor history of open hiring and recruitment practices that they look for "triple headers" — that is, employees who can be counted three times on required government documents related to affirmative action. If you have any traits that are related to affirmative-action hiring, specify these traits in your cover letter. (Despite claims to the contrary, employers are still free to hire the most qualified applicants.)

The Interview

If you are called in for an interview, prepare for it. Most organizations consider the interview to be the most important part of the employee-selection process. From your point of view, the interview may be a tension-producing event. The knowledge that an interview has been scheduled is enough to cause stomach problems for some people. If you have been scheduled for an interview, the organization has seen a set of talents and skills in your application that might match its needs. You have already passed one screening before the interview takes place. Let's look at the pressures surrounding an interview situation:

> The organization is always faced with balancing its desire to attract the best people with its desire to gather valid selection data. The typical interview is a microcosm of these competing desires. Part of the time the interviewer is in the role of attracting the person, and part of the time he is in the role of trying to evaluate the person. This conflict can produce obvious stress and strain in the interviewer. The situation faced by the interviewer is similar to that faced by the job applicant who tries to both attract the organization and gather information about it. In a sense, deciding how to behave in the selection situation is a game played by both the organization and the job applicant, and how each one plays it depends on where he perceives he stands with respect to the other at that moment. How each one plays it also has a very strong influence on the likelihood that the selection process will result in a decision that is good for both the applicant and the organization (Lawler, 1973:100).

Rather than let the tension build until the day and hour of the interview, you should do your homework. You already know a bit about the organization, but you should continue your research. Make sure you have at least two questions to ask your interviewers.

When the day of the interview arrives, be prompt, neat, and polite. Listen closely, and be sure to remember the interviewer's name, calling him or her by a title (i.e. Mr., Mrs., Dr., etc.) and last name unless directed otherwise. *Look the interviewer in the eye at least once during the interview.* If it is a group interview, try to establish eye contact with each person in the group. Don't slouch, but do try to be somewhat relaxed. If you feel anxious during the interview, try leaning against the back of the chair rather than constantly sitting on the edge. It's likely that the chair you sit in will be lower than your prospective employer's chair, and a large desk will provide the interviewer with a sense of security, while you sit with nothing in front of you but your legs and feet. You may be nervous, especially if you really want the job, but remember that the interview wasn't designed to make you uncomfortable.

If you are asked a question that you don't understand or can't answer, say "I'm not sure I understand that question. Could you ask it in a different way?" Nine times out of ten, the person who asked the question will either give you a clue to the answer or try to rephrase the question. If the interview is interrupted by a visitor or a telephone call, focus on the topic that was being discussed when the interruption occurred. As soon as the interruption is over, say something like "Before we were interrupted we were talking about. . . ."

Silence causes most people to feel uncomfortable, including the person who is interviewing you. The questions that you had planned before the interview can be asked during any uncomfortable pauses. These questions really serve two purposes; they can fill unwanted silences and, at the same time, allow you to interview the interviewer. Questions that relate to something said earlier in the interview indicate your ability to listen and recall. The following is an example of such a question. "Earlier you said you had worked here for five years. What major attributes of this organization attracted you during that period?"

Planned questions can help you determine the organization's philosophy of helping. A question such as "What are the major strengths of your clients?" may elicit responses varying from shock to a description of an agency's philosophy. When you are asked if there is anything else you want to say, you should ask your heaviest question, if you haven't already. Examples are: "What would you judge to be the major two or three problems that your organization now faces?" and "What do you see as the major changes that need to be made to improve the organization's service?"

The First Three Months

Often, new workers are frantic and impatient workers. They forget that the process of growing, learning, healing—changing in any way—is both complex and natural. You took the job as a human-service worker to help people through this process.

You may soon discover that most of your coworkers don't seem to feel the same way you do. Before you make harsh judgments of more experienced workers, and before you begin to give your clients all you've got, use some of your energy to get to know the organization for which you work. Hoffer (1967:4), longshoreman turned professor, made the classic observation that workers who are sure of their skills go leisurely about their jobs and accomplish much; they work as though they are at play. Many individuals beginning careers in human services attack their work as though they were saving the world. Remember, your clients had their needs before you arrived.

The Organization's Norms

You can get to know an organization by becoming familiar with its *norms*. Norms are unwritten rules and guidelines that are understood and followed by the members of a group. Student nurses are taught that the patient-care plan is a carefully conceived, well-written document that should be developed by all of the staff members on the floor. They are told that the plan should provide the basis for conferences in which the staff members discuss each of the patients. However, most hospitals don't follow this procedure. Some schools contain more than one teachers' lounge; one of the lounges may only be for a selected group of faculty members. In a public health clinic, the physical exams may not include blood samples, even though these are required by the federal government. In a mental hospital, television programs may be selected by the patients according to formal rules; however, a complex system may exist whereby staff members bribe selected patients to tune in the programs that the staff wants to watch. Working in a prison, guards may discover that regardless of the situation, they should never accept [cigarette] lights from inmates, because that gesture is associated with bribery. You may find that even when the supervisor's office door is open, you are expected to knock before you enter.

These practices and rules are all examples of norms. The more norms you can identify in an organization, the more productive and satisfied you will be in that organization. How many reports, observations, lesson plans, tickets, or memos are you expected to complete each week? Do the other workers fall behind in their work, or do they stay late or come early to see clients, catch up, and complete paperwork?

Even though you want to prove that you are a competent, hardworking employee, you should find out what is considered an acceptable work rate before you give it all you've got. A new employee is not usually disciplined for being too slow. The organization that hired you expects that it will take time for you to learn your job. Experienced employees may, however, chastise you if you "break the rate" even though you may be doing so out of ignorance. After you've learned what the work rate is, you'll know what is expected of you and be less likely to violate an important norm by accident. You can then ask yourself, "Do I go along with the norm?" This question is one that you will have to face as long as you work in a human-service organization with others doing the same job.

Conflict Between You and the Norms

You know what is right for yourself. You've been trained, schooled, and educated, and you know how to do your job. The difference between what you know *should* be and what you actually find will cause many conflicts.

Here, an established employee (a security guard) describes one early experience:

> We had what we called 'lock up.' Whenever there was something going on, the kids were locked in their rooms. This was the rule that the superintendent thought was a must—the way you should deal with kids who are to be locked up from the courts. I didn't really think too much of that rule. It created a lot of dissension between me and the kids. It really made a lot of work for me, and I kinda rebelled against that. But I managed to find other ways to get kids out from being locked up. I always had some kind of a job or cleanup—something for the kids to do that I could use to keep them out of their rooms. I had a heck of a lot more cooperation from the kids. I did not have the fighting, confusion, broken windows, ripped up toilet stools, and that kind of stuff.
>
> Before long, I had what looked like a happy group of kids in our wing. The other guys [security men] couldn't quite really understand or figure out what I was doing—why I had such a quiet wing. I was called on the carpet a couple of times about how come my boys were always out when they should have been locked up. Each time, I told them that my kids had work to do. This seemed to satisfy my supervisors; it hadn't created any security risk, and it did keep things quiet. The other guys working with me saw what was happening. They had a hard time buying it, because they were strictly 'lock up and forget it.' Finally, they realized that, if they let the kids out and kept them

busy, they could have a quiet wing too and an easier day for themselves as well as for the kids. I think I better elaborate a little more on this. I think I better tell you about 'bending the rules.' If you feel you have to put a little kink in a rule, you just don't kink it to kink it; you'd better evaluate it and look at it closely when you finally decide that you are going to bend it. You have to use good judgment and common sense. I really got lucky on this one.

An example of a conflict between established rules and the behavior of coworkers is described in the following anecdote. This employee had been placed on the night shift as the lone attendant in a security tower, where he was armed with a rifle:

During the first month or so in the tower, the lieutenant constantly called me up and wanted to know what was going on. He was really checking to see whether I was awake. As part of his nightly duties, he would go to the far corner of the yard to feed the dogs twice a night. It was an institution rule that any employee who was in the yard at night would flash a light, and I was to flash an acknowledgment. He was then to flash me back. I would flash him and he wouldn't flash me in return. This happened for about two or three days, and I finally said the heck with it. I didn't flash him. Then he began to flash me. I would flash him back, but he wouldn't flash me back. This happened for a couple of days; then he proceeded in the same way — he would not flash. I would flash and he wouldn't acknowledge. Then it got to the point where I wouldn't flash and he would call me up and want to know if I was awake. He told me to stay with it, or else. So one night I decided there had to be something done in order to change this man's attitude. I knew he was coming down to feed the dogs at an approximate time. I unloaded the 30-30, and I waited for him to come into sight. It was about 4:00 A.M. I remember the night air was real still. As he came around the corner to feed the dogs, I flashed him. He didn't flash me in any way, or acknowledge in any way, so I opened the door to the tower, stepped out on the ledge, lifted the bolt on the rifle, put the flashlight on the barrel, and pointed it in the direction of the dogs. The hammer clicked in the night air. He flashed me immediately, and, from that point on, he called me up every time to let me know he was going down to feed the dogs.

Conflicts can be seen as opportunities to change and grow, to bargain and reconcile, and to compete and mediate. Before you tackle the resolution of any conflict, you should consider two major items: (1) a set of priorities and (2) a personal-support system. Priorities may be listed in several ways. One list might reflect the degree of difficulty; another might indicate how long it will take to resolve each conflict; a third might detail the "actors," their positions in the organization, and their relationships to one another. (You can think of this last list as limited sociogram.) A final list could rank conflicts according to their importance to you. Your task is to combine these lists. It is not unusual to discover that the various lists interlock. The conflicts that you have identified will most likely form a web. It is not usually possible to tackle one conflict without becoming involved with the others.

After you've made some tentative choices about where you should begin, consider your personal-support systems. What resources will you need? Are those resources available to you? One of your most important resources will be the psychological support of your coworkers. A spouse, a friend, or a roommate may provide a viewpoint that you have not considered. Those who value and respect you and your skills become even more important when the going gets rough.

Conflicts are not often quickly and easily resolved. Conflict only occurs in the context of interdependence, therefore, you and the things that are causing you trouble are dependent on each other to some extent. You might be tempted to isolate yourself from "them" or "it." The results of such a strategy of isolation are most likely visible in your organization. Poor communication is only one negative result of isolation. More damaging to the organization in the long run, is that supervisors may see the absence of conflict as a sign that cooperation is taking place. In terms of service delivery, such an assumption can be damaging to both the staff and the clients. Isolation postpones the resolution of conflicts and often acts to magnify the original problems. The solution of most human problems takes time. You have to keep working, even though you may be working in a less-than-ideal situation. A former student of mine puts it this way:

> As I began my job in a training school for the mentally handicapped, I realized that all of the 500 residents needed some sort of help. Fresh out of college and full of ideas, I really felt that I could help in making some changes in their lives. Then the "system" became evident to me, and the frustration of not being able to make progress became overwhelming. Everything I started became bogged down with paperwork, policies, and apathetic coworkers. It soon occurred to me that attempting to change the entire setup was unrealistic. So, I began to single out specific residents with specific problems and concentrated my efforts on them. I was then told by my supervisors and coworkers that I was playing favorites. But, by channeling my efforts on one resident at a time, I could actually see some positive results over

a period of time. When one child learned to walk alone, or learned to feed himself, or was placed in a home setting, all the hassle was worthwhile.

Some conflicts may seem simple; make sure you have all the information you need before you attempt to find resolutions. For example, it is foolish to criticize an established employee before you know all of the details. Genuine compliments are usually accepted by coworkers. Questions asked of carefully selected coworkers usually are answered. Most staff members with whom I've worked—especially teachers—don't go up the line for help; they ask other staff members at the same level. Being a student or trainee yesterday and a staff member today can be a shock. You may not be sure whether you'll sink or swim. Some of the other staff members at your level have had years of experience. Some of them will be willing to let you benefit from their experience; others will expect you to sink or swim on your own. A new prison guard had this experience:

> I can recall the first night I worked the yard detail. I had an officer—an old officer who had been there approximately fifteen years—and, as we started the yard trip for the clock run, I told the officer that I was new on the assignment and that he would have to explain where we were going and what we were doing. He told me I would learn the same way he did. Nobody told him, and he wasn't about to tell me. And so that was the way it was. I just watched, and when it came time for my turn to take the yard watch by myself, I just had to play it by ear.

Your clients are subject to norms as well. In many ways, they have a more difficult job than you in discovering unwritten rules. High school students quickly learn formal rules. They learn that they must walk up the "up" staircases and down the "down" staircases. They must not run in the halls. They must not be late to classes. They even learn complex traffic patterns, such as the changing one-way directions of certain hallways during certain times of the day. At the same time, the students learn informal laws, or norms. They must not cut in front of a teacher in the lunch line or smoke in certain areas. These kinds of norms are relatively easy to learn.

There is a more complex set of norms that depend on the particular staff person involved. Don't call a teacher by his or her first name when that teacher, or another teacher, can hear you. Though school rules specify that students are not to be late to class; students quickly learn that some teachers allow a 30-second leniency before they count a student as tardy. Some teachers always allow a few minutes near the end of the class period for talking or studying. Some teachers do not give homework over weekends and holidays. Usually, teachers who establish these kinds of norms (which are understood by the student) expect something in return, such as good behavior when a supervisor is in the room or when a substitute teacher takes over the class. These kinds of unwritten contracts between staff and clients are discovered slowly and are never openly discussed. The skillfulness with which we can discern these contracts is a tribute to human ingenuity.

Perceptive clients quickly learn whether or not you are the kind of person with whom they can crack a joke and under what conditions you will accept and approve of this kind of behavior. Clients learn, for instance, that they can trade jokes with you only when there are no other staff members present. Licata and Willower (1975) have studied *student brinkmanship*—that is, the art of driving teachers crazy without getting into trouble. The testing of authority is familiar to anyone who has ever sat in a classroom. The skill level of the clients determines how sophisticated this testing becomes. In the late 1930s, Hayner and Ash (1939) conducted one of the first studies on prison inmates. They describe the complex process of producing coffee in prison cells. They conclude this description by saying, "The successful evasion of a rule is even more satisfying than the finished product." The process by which clients find out what makes you tick is very complex and systematic; the outcome of that process will, in part, determine how effective you are at your job.

Generations of human-service workers have fought the good fight and made some significant improvements; however, there is still much that needs to be done. Nurses discover that they cannot do the kind of nursing for which they were trained because of the very large patient/nurse ratio. "When you come out and you're the R.N., you're probably put in as a charge nurse and you simply just don't have the time to give the total patient care that you were taught." A beginning teacher is torn between the desire to change the outdated methods and attitudes toward education and the need for the department chairperson's approval.

Feedback

After a few weeks, you'll probably wonder how you're doing on the job. You may begin to feel that you're not doing well, because nobody has said anything about your work. You need reliable feedback in order to evaluate yourself and your performance. Sometimes a straight question addressed to your supervisor will elicit a straight answer. Carefully chosen coworkers may be another source of feedback, but staff members may not tell you what you want to know.

You may have found a coworker you can really trust. Perhaps an established worker who wants to help you will give you a Dutch Uncle Talk—that is, something like, "What really counts around here are the papers in your file, not the service you give to the clients. The promotions, the raises, and the vacation time come from the bureaucracy in the organization, not from the clients. We do it this way here." The purpose of such a talk is to make you face the fact that your expectations and personal values may not match the expectations and values of the organization for which you work. If, after being confronted with these differences, you use your own values and beliefs, more drastic action may be taken. A psychiatric aide had this experience:

> The patients' luncheon used to come on food elevators, and I was one of the people who were to pick them out, prepare to serve them, and then serve them after the patients came to pick their food. There were usually two or three other psychiatric aides besides me. Most of the food that was for the patients was awfully big pieces. The food would come up, and they would line up, and we would have to serve them one by one. One of the first shocking things that I was asked to do was to throw away about 15 uneaten hamburgers and open three or four quarts of unopened milk cartons and throw them all in the garbage disposal. Having come from a starving nation, I was really shocked. I protested, but the nursing supervisor told me that there was no point in sending the food down, because this would mean more of a problem for the kitchen people, who would then have to store the food back. And so I had better throw all of these uneaten hamburgers and unopened cartons of milk in the garbage disposal. Once, I did return some of those milk cartons back to the kitchen only to find at the next meal they did not send any milk up.

Humor and sarcasm are often used to tell newcomers that they have violated a norm. A secondary-school teacher reports such an incident:

> My first year I was really gung-ho with my room. I tried to decorate the bulletin boards and make displays. Well, people thought this was hilarious. They kept telling me that I should go and teach second grade if I liked doing this. I did it anyway. One day I just decided I had enough. Someone stuck their head in and said something very sarcastic. I said, "If more people around here would decorate their rooms, the kids might be more willing to come and sit in that class for an hour and a half." I needed help that first year. I didn't need someone to come in and laugh at me.

Adjustment to Failure

Adjustment to failure is a central part of a new employee's socialization process. This adjustment is difficult, because the new employee is usually fired up with spirit and idealism. After all, you have been successful throughout your educational career and your internship has probably been successful. You probably have a firm desire to be humanistic, concerned, and considerate to all your clients. Consequently, when a client fails to respond to your efforts, you experience a sense of failure. The following poem describes the feelings of a beginning English teacher:

> The school room is dark, and a womb that knows no birth
> But dies and dies again, no birth, no life to give
> To John or Jane. A factual facade
> Caresses tight and lets no living in.
> The teacher only lives a dream of know.
> He hides behind the is or cannot be
> And fails to hear and see the I and me
> That sits behind the silent crying eyes.
> But sometimes when the sun cracks through those stones
> That keep the touch of outside from the in
> The radiant hopes of sunshine kisses warm
> Despite a touch of maybe through the walls.
> And golden raindrops smooth and soft and sheer
> Caress and free those dreams that still may live.

Summary

Perhaps you have a job that involves helping people or are considering such a job. In this chapter, guidelines are offered on job selection, application, and interview behavior. Maybe you'll apply and be interviewed. If a "matchup" occurs between your talents and needs and an organization's requirements, you'll take the job and work with a group of employees. Since the day you entered kindergarten, you have been a newcomer to groups. You have experienced the tension before, but somehow this is different. The work situation probably won't turn out to be quite what you expected it to be.

Helping is hard work. Once you've been trained to help clients, your biggest problems will be with your coworkers and the rules, regulations, policies, procedures, and traditions of the organization for which you work.

Your job environment contains dedicated staff members, helpful supervisors, and appreciative clients. If you focus too much energy on the negative aspects of your workplace, you may lack the energy you need to do your job and maintain your own mental and physical health. Your mental health and professional responsibilities require you to maintain a balance.

Discussion Questions

1. What is your personal-support system? Whom do you go to for help?
2. What physical place or places in your life feel most comfortable to you?
3. What are the norms that operate in your classroom or present work situation? For example, for the former, make a list of norms regarding attendance, verbal participation, and relationships with instructors. For the latter, describe the norms associated with work rate, coffee or other refreshment use, the staff lounge area, dress codes, and so on.
4. Which of these norms are nonproductive? How could you change them?
5. Name several philosophies of helping. Describe the assumptions about clients inherent in each of these philosophies.
6. Describe your philosophy of helping.

References

Bernstein, G. S., and Halaszyn, J. A. 1989. *Human Services? . . . That Must be so Rewarding*. Baltimore: Paul H. Brookes Publishing Co.

Hayner, N. S., and Ash, E. 1939. The prisoner community as a social group. *American Sociological Review*, 4, 362-69.

Hoffer, E. 1967. *The Ordeal of Change*. New York: Harper & Row.

Lawler, E. E., III. 1973. *Motivation in Work Organizations*. Monterey, CA: Brooks/Cole.

Sheridan, J. E., Richards, M. D., and Slocom, J. W. 1975. Comparative analysis of expectancy and heuristic models of decision behavior. *Journal of Applied Psychology*, 60, 361-68.

Vroom, V. H., and Deci, E. L. 1971. The stability of post decisional dissonance: A follow-up study of job attitude of business school graduates. *Organizational Behavior and Human Performance*, 6, 36-49.

Wanous, J. P. 1975. *Organizational Entry: The Transition from Outsider to Newcomer to Insider*. Working paper 75-14. New York University, Graduate School of Business Administration.

2 The People

The people your organization helps — clients, students, inmates, or wards — are the reason for your job. They have their own view of you, their own view of all the other people who are employed by your organization, and their own view of one another. Clients have a lot of things in common with you, and with one another, because you're all human. People need air, water, food, physical security, psychological security, acceptance, love, opportunity for growth, and the need to be needed by another human being. Jourard (1964), Maslow (1962), May (1950), and O'Banion and O'Connell (1970) are a few of the well known psychologists who have written somewhat poetically about human needs. Each of them has a special set of words to tell us how we feel; however, we don't need psychologists to tell us about loneliness or what it feels like to be hurt by a partner. Toffler (1970) documents this fact in *Future Shock*. Bernstein and Halaszyn (1989) stress that we tend to devalue people when we focus only on their problems as is so easy to do in a client/staff relationship. We all have problems but we are still entitled to respect and recognition for our contributions.

Clients

The need to be important — to count — is felt by all of us, including the clients and staff members with whom you work. If you look carefully at each person as an individual, you will see behavior that indicates this need. The need to be recognized as a human being is sometimes so strong in people who have been consistently ignored that it comes out in bizarre ways. Mental patients often demonstrate this need dramatically. A psychiatric worker describes the following incidents:

> Half the problems arise out of sheer desperation. They need attention so bad sometimes, they want somebody to talk to so bad that they walk up and down, up and down, up and down. The morning shift ought to ask, 'What's wrong, Harold?' Nobody asks. Harold walks by three or four times and finally he gets angry. He knocks the ashtray over. Then everybody comes jumping around to catch him and give him a shot. Harold's happy. He's smiling. He's got all the attention. Another patient would break windows and cut herself up just to get attention. She'd be really happy with the doctor patching her up. Then she'd wander. Sometimes they'd give her a shot, but she wouldn't lie down, or she'd get out of bed and punch through another window. So they'd tell me to sit in her window, and they'd tie her down. Later, when she was untied, this girl starts stripping, and she's really beautiful. She'd sit and she'd masturbate in front of me.

Maybe you've never experienced anything like this, but you can remember the kid at school who was the expert brinkman — the one who could push the rules to the fine line. The books falling on the floor by "accident," the feigned cough, the loud laughter, all take place in front of an audience. These things are all disguised in order to keep the culprit out of real trouble. The profanity is always spoken in a low voice, but loud enough for the other students to hear. Willower (Licata and Willower, 1975) found that students do these things in school not only to demonstrate their skill but also to get attention from other people.

Your clients are people in the system who are trying to meet their needs. Because their behavior may demand much of your attention; you may forget that they are a lot like you. This is especially true of new staff members, because, except in unusual circumstances, new employees are assigned to the toughest clients, the slowest classes, the least desirable shift, the hardest caseload, the most boring work station, and the least convenient schedule. A beginning teacher puts it this way:

> I had five different classes, each with a different preparation. All but one of these classes was in the lowest track. Oh, the chairman — well, she teaches an honors English and two accelerated English classes.

In many general hospitals, beginning nurses work the evening shift. One nurse explained this phenomenon:

> It's the shift that has the least help. You have as much to do as you do on days, but you have less people and it's hard to get a hold of doctors, partly because you know they are not coming in. Also, you hesitate to call them, because, being on evenings, you don't really get to know the doctors who usually make their rounds in the morning.

A new prison guard thought he could select the shift he wanted:

> I told him [the captain] that I didn't care to go on the night shift — that I would prefer to stay on the day shift. He told me that it was up to me: either I went on the night shift or I went out the door, so the choice was not that large. I was on the night shift for about a year, and I worked almost all assignments on the night shift. I worked cell houses, front and back barracks, the towers, the yard watch, the guard hall, and the arsenal.

You want to help the clients. You may seek help from more experienced staff members. If you are frustrated in your attempts to obtain help in one-to-one talks with coworkers, you might decide to try to get help for your clients in a more formal situation, like a staff meeting:

> In the teacher meetings that we would have, I would mention things that I would like to do with my class. Once, I asked about team teaching. Another teacher and I tried this, and right away we were told it was out. I tried to talk about how I felt about my kids, the things they did and how I tried to deal with them. I got the feeling that people were talking behind my back and, at times, saying things like 'Follow the rules and don't cause any trouble or try to change anything, because we don't want to have to do it.'

An institutional nurse, in discussing the fact that some of the students needed eyeglasses, tried to get help through her supervisor. Later, she brought up the issue at a staff meeting and received this answer:

> 'We don't do things like that here. Our budget isn't set up for that.' And when I'd ask, 'Well, who is *we?*', nobody could tell me who we was. So, between 'We've never done it that way' and 'We've always done it this way,' I hit one brick wall after another.

The clients you confront will behave in ways that may seem very confusing. They will try to find out as quickly as possible what kind of a person you are and how far you're going to go in meeting their needs. Some things clients need can not be paid for out of regular budgets. For example, in the typical state agency, budget lines for materials and supplies for direct use by clients are usually limited.

Attempts to help clients in ways that are outside established rules can take a variety of forms. A staff member working on a chronic ward in a state run mental health center reports:

> Sometimes we have money-making projects like cake sales. Presently, we have a monthly dinner, the proceeds of which go to the patients' fund. We buy such things as a hair dryer for the women on the ward and cigarettes and soda for those who don't have any money. A simple thing like a comb is very often the hardest thing to come across. Many packs of cigarettes, soda, coffee, and combs are bought for patients by employees on the ward. Each employee decides just how generous to be and how often to be "taken." The results of this are that some of the patients have begun to expect such presents in the normal course of events. When some of us don't feel we have the personal funds to do these kind of things, the patients respond to us like we really didn't care about them. Even though we meant to do good, I think this kind of activity has interfered with our treatment program.

When clients are in a group, they seek to gain acceptance and status among their peers. Prison inmates test a new correctional officer. Ambulatory hospital patients try to see how many doors they can get you to unlock with your new set of keys. Detention-home residents want to find out how many extra telephone calls you will allow them to place. Students, prison inmates, patients, and residents all need to know how flexible you are willing to be on the institutional time schedule. Do you start class on time, turn out the lights when you're supposed to, do bed check thoroughly and on time, stay to see they have taken their medicine, and adhere to other routine institutional matters? They need to know what, if any, changes you plan to make in either the written or the unwritten rules.

The clients have had experience with a number of other authority figures, and they have learned how to live with them. In this sense, they have an advantage, especially if this is the first time you have been in a position of authority. They are experienced, and you are not. If you choose to make it a battle the odds are with them, not only because they are more experienced but also because they outnumber you. Jacobs, a criminologist, and Retsky, a former prison guard turned counselor, describe the ways in which inmates can jeopardize a guard's job, for example, by messing up the "count" — the counting process that takes place several times a day (Jacobs and Retsky, 1975).

Braswell, Fletcher, and Miller (1990) present an array of "cons" that have been pulled on prison employees. When you get "conned," you will likely feel a combination of betrayal, frustration, and embarrassment.

On the other hand, if you see the situation as an opportunity to learn and for the clients to help you learn, the chance of your relationship with clients becoming a battle of wills is reduced. The danger in this attitude, however, is that the clients may seduce you into becoming so concerned about their personal welfare that you lose your effectiveness. Jacobs (1974) discusses the consequences when a new correctional officer takes on the role of a counselor. In the belief that he is helping the rehabilitation process, the new guard takes the correctional process into his own hands by allowing the inmates more privileges than the rules allow. According to Jacobs, the consequences of this arrangement are usually negative.

In most correctional institutions, the security officers use a system of written reports, or "tickets," to describe inmate misbehavior. These tickets may lead to a form of punishment, such as the revocation of a previously earned privilege. An inmate told a new guard that he was going to kill him. The guard chose not to write a ticket:

> Instead of that, I tried to calm him down. I tried to talk to him for most of the rest of my shift. He didn't want to talk, so, just before I left, I wrote up a ticket and turned it in. The next morning, as soon as I got to work, the inmate called me to his cell and apologized. We had a good discussion. He gave me a lot of commitments. I told him I would drop the ticket and simply write up an incident report, which would go into his jacket [file] but wouldn't be considered a disciplinary violation. I went to the captain's office to have him drop the ticket so I could write an incident report. The captain told me he didn't have the power to let me take the ticket back—I would have to talk to the unit commander. The unit commander refused to let me dismiss the ticket and said that all violations are punished. I then called the warden in charge of security, and he said the ticket would be handled and processed. It was out of my hands. The inmate went to the hole for 15 days. I was in a bad light with the captain, the unit commander, and the warden. When the inmate came out, he said he held no hard feelings, but he seemed apathetic about the whole deal.

> This incident was followed by another poor judgment on my part. Two men had been killed in the cell house on _____. Very soon thereafter, five security officers were taken hostage in the cell unit for about three hours but released unharmed. The warden put the whole institution in dead lock [all inmates

locked in their cells 24 hours a day]. Our unit had not been involved in either of these incidents, and I thought it was unjust. Our unit shouldn't be treated like all of the rest. The warden and the unit commander told me they felt the same way and told me that, if the rest of the guards on our unit agreed, he would not put our men on dead lock. I put it to a vote. I was the only vote to let them out. This got me off to a bad start with the other guards but got me a lot of help from the inmates. One example was that a fairly new inmate tried to give me a hard time one day about trying to get into his cell, and the rest of the men told him to quit giving me a hard time.

As I look back now, my behavior in both of these incidents has been one of the major factors in my not being promoted. The chief guard and my lieutenant have blocked every promotion that I have tried to get in the last three-and-a-half years.

Your Feelings About Clients

Do you dislike your clients because of the way they behave? Do you disapprove of your clients' behavior but still accept them as human beings? The people you're there to help need to know what kinds of things threaten you and what kinds of things you can deal with in a fair and objective manner. If you're not sure yourself, it will help you to find out. A personal journal in which you describe feelings about each day's or night's work will give you some clues about your fears and your ability to deal with problems. I encourage you to experiment with the form of your journal.

Here are a few suggestions that some people have found useful. Use a hardbound book that opens flat for easier writing. Paperback and loose-leaf books aren't very durable. A few key questions may help to guide you in your entries. You could write a factual description of each day's events, filling in the actors, the circumstances, and the outcomes. What did you do? What actions, if any, did you take? What alternatives did you have in the situation? You may find it helpful to use your journal for self-examination at the end of each week, month, or pay period. Ask yourself questions such as "What kinds of clients attract me?", "Which clients repel me?", "What do I like most about what I am doing?", and "What do I like least about my job?"

The most important question to be answered in your daily journal is "How did I *feel* about what happened?" This is the hardest part for most of us. Feelings and emotions drive our behavior. *Sad, glad, happy, excited, disgusted, revolted, thrilled, anxious, pleased, warm,* and *angry* are words that should appear in your journal.

Dealing with Clients

As a human-service worker, you may find yourself in a situation in which the majority of those with whom you work really want help, but a very vocal minority constantly interferes with your efforts. In such a situation, how would you continue to help the majority and deal with the disruptive influence of those who appear to be saying "We don't want your help"? Maybe you will be forced to separate one group from the other until the majority is willing and able to help you control the "troublemakers." You may be good at your job, but you can't do all things for all people. The facts are that most inmates return to prison, many hospitalized mental patients are repeaters, delinquents can con you, some students don't want to learn, and clients aren't always truthful.

In the more typical case, in which the entire group seems to be saying "We will tolerate you if you will tolerate us, but don't make changes or demands," the decision for you is much clearer. Some client groups, especially in institutions, will seem to say, "If you don't bother us, we won't bother you." Smith and Geoffrey (1968:151) calls this "the contract" when they talk about classrooms. These kinds of contracts are never written down, but students and teachers know what's expected. Some clients have discovered that the way to get out is to be "rehabilitated." These clients may say, "Tell us the rules of the game, and we will play." They learn exactly what you want and how you want it. They choose to play to get what they want — grades, welfare checks, or release. These clients have adjusted to an involuntary situation. They understand both the written and the unwritten rules, and they have learned, in their own way, how to live with them.

While your clients are trying to find out what makes you tick, you're trying to discover the most effective means of dealing with them. This tendency to "psych each other out" is especially strong during your first contacts; the tension produced by this process dissipates over time. Again, if you choose to make it a battle, the clients have a big advantage. As you try to psych out the clients, you are also trying to learn about your coworkers, your immediate supervisor, and the organization that has hired you. When the clients push you during that first contact, stand your ground without being belligerent. If you choose to fight the clients, they will probably win. Perhaps you are thinking, "No, I can beat them at this first skirmish, and I'm going to find out what makes them tick and be able to hide who I really am from them." However, your victory will be a temporary one. The clients will quickly learn how you do battle, and they probably won't make the same mistakes twice. The kind of attitude that has helped new staff members is illustrated by an institutional nurse:

> All the employees here represent to that boy everybody that's helped to put him in this place. We personify the teacher he couldn't get along with, the cop who busted him, the probation officer who gave up on him, the judge who sentenced him, the state's attorney who prosecuted him, and even the transportation officer who brought him here. He has an extremely touchy sense of justice. Just the fact that another boy might have a bigger scoop of ice cream is an injustice. Once you're in tune with these feelings, I think it's easier to understand the kid. [The] administration divorces themselves from the everyday happenings in an institution. They send down a few memos here and there with a bunch of rules and regulations that you kind of have to work around. Our administrators don't even begin to understand this superfine sense of justice and injustice. I think actual helping starts after there is some mutual feeling, good and sometimes even bad, but honest feeling expressed—a little bit of trust starting to develop and the fact that the boy knows that you're going to be fair, that you're going to give him a fair shake.

Those of you who work on a one-to-one basis will go through a similar process with clients as they test you. For example, a mother receiving Aid to Families with Dependent Children (AFDC) may coach her children before you arrive. As a result, when you ask questions such as "Where is your father?" or "When does your mother get home from work?", the answers will be designed to maximize the amount of the next check. Most likely, the lies are not meant personally. You are seen as a representative of the system. The clients' survival depends on their ability to work with, and if necessary, take advantage of the system. The AFDC mother may have dealt with other caseworkers before you; in that sense, she is more experienced than you are.

Similar examples are provided by mental-health workers who are hustled by drug-dependent clients. The workers may discover that they have helped to secure a prescription from the supervising psychiatrist for a client's favorite drug. Even worse, the client may have taken advantage of the new relationship with a worker to steal a pad of prescription blanks. It hurts to discover that you have been used. Your first response to such behavior may be to feel hurt and deceived. Unless you put these experiences in a larger context, a series of such events may lead you to become cynical.

According to your personal set of values and beliefs, deception may be wrong. You probably don't hurt people who are trying to help you. The client's values may differ from your own. For instance, the client may believe that deception is a profitable skill to be learned and practiced, and that people who represent the system are there to be used. Such values are likely to contradict your own.

Just as your behavior is guided by your beliefs and values, so too is the client's. One of your tasks may be to help the client change his or her values. Altering values and belief systems is usually a long-term process. Are you patient enough to endure the feeling of being used in order to demonstrate a different value system?

Staff Members

Many established employees at all staff levels come across as cruel, indifferent, or incompetent. These employees may have been burned out by a series of events. At one time, they may have been a lot like you are now. Their words and actions may seem shocking to you as they talk about clients and treat them poorly. A youth supervisor in an institution for delinquents said, "When I first started working, we had rules that dealt with kids as if they were animals, something you take and throw away. Just lock them up and forget about them." A psychiatric aide recalled that he was told to treat patients as normal people, but he saw most of the staff treating the patients as though they were little children. In your work you will probably see behavior that will repulse you; it may encourage you to do something to change what is happening right away. These next examples dramatically describe the abuses that can occur in systems that process large numbers of people. In such systems, some people are inevitably neglected and abused. A psychiatric hospital nurse reports the following:

> A patient had fallen off his bed and hit his head. He was dead the next day when they found him. What happened was, when they made the morning head count, they looked around casually and couldn't find him. They made out a report saying that he was missing from the ward. That day they didn't find him. At 5:00 P.M. they made another report saying that they couldn't find him and he'd run away. The next day, the morning shift came and checked off that he was not on the ward because he had run away. Sometime in the afternoon, they found him by the side of the bed dead . . . in the pool of blood. And they called me and

another guy to move him. All the blood had matted and he had rigor mortis.

A newly hired correctional officer described the following experience:

> About four of us officers and two lieutenants were taken back to the segregation area and told an inmate had grabbed an officer in charge of the segregation area, taken his cigarettes and his glasses, and that we would have to go into his cell and get these materials out. When we got to the man's cell, they gave me a blanket and told me that the lieutenant would go in first, hit the inmate in the stomach, and try to tackle him, and that I would throw a blanket over the man's head and we would try to restrain him this way. We took off our glasses, ties, and hats, and went into the man's cell. I remember feeling anxious and scared about what was going to happen. I really didn't know what I was supposed to do. The inmate was backed up into the corner of his cell, and so, as the gate [door] was opened, it was somewhat dark in the cell. As the gate was opened, the lieutenant ran in. I ran in behind him and [tried to] slip the blanket over the man's head—he happened to be about six foot five. I could neither reach his head nor throw the blanket over it. I tried my best, finally dropping the blanket and grabbing the man by the head. We pulled the man down and we had him restrained to where we could get the material from him, but this was not enough.
>
> The next few minutes in that cell made me very, very sick for about a day afterwards. I saw the lieutenant, who had been working with me on the night shift. As we were holding the man, he came with a blackjack in his hand and proceeded to beat the man on the head seriously, accidentally hitting me several times. The man's [lieutenant's] eyes dilated, and he seemed to thoroughly enjoy hitting the inmate. Finally, another lieutenant had to pull him off. The inmate all the time was hollering "Quit—please, I quit. Don't hurt me." When we left the cell, the man was laying on the floor, and I had a severe stomachache.

A psychiatric aide described an experience in which a patient jumped on him:

> Other staff hurdled the patient off and started hitting him and told me to hit him. The patient just looked around. You could have hit him all day and he wouldn't have done anything. I took him to bed and I put him down. Then I saw another employee hit him real hard, and the guy went down and hit his head against the bed. He got a big cut on his head and they had to call the doctor to get stitches. He was walking with a limp. They said that he fell over and hit his bed.

A new prison guard reported the following experience:

> I was called to the segregation department, where an inmate who
> had been causing a disturbance refused to come out of a cell.
> A white man was in segregation with a group of blacks and had
> been calling them names and threatening them. He wasn't able
> to get to them nor they to him, but it was causing total frustration
> within the unit. The man had to be moved into a quieter
> segregation area, where he could not hurt someone or tear up
> his cell. When we went to get him, he had a paper sack over his
> head, but cut open so he could breathe. He knew that we would
> be coming in with mace. The captain tried to talk him out. The
> man refused and backed into the corner of his cell, holding a
> broom handle, and told us we'd have to take him out. The captain
> again tried to reason with the man, but to no avail. He then
> sprayed him with tear gas mace until the man pulled off the
> paper sack. He [the captain] sprayed some more, but this didn't
> stop the man. When we opened the cell to go in, the captain and
> the lieutenant went in. It was one of our more violent lieutenants.
> He got just clipped with the broom and he backed off. The
> captain tackled the inmate, and I grabbed him by the head. I
> got the inmate down on the bed, and he gave up immediately.
> The captain and I were covered with tear gas, and it made it very
> hard for us to see. We got the handcuffs and the lead chains on
> the inmate and put the chain between his legs and led him out
> of the cell.
>
> After we got him out on the gallery, the lieutenant grabbed the
> inmate by the hair and hit him five to seven times in the face.
> The captain and I stood there. Nothing was said. When he
> stopped, we took the inmate to isolation and put him in another
> cell. Then I had to make a written report. Also, the captain and
> lieutenants had to make a report on what happened in moving
> the inmate. I was told by the captain to write 'minimum restraint
> was required in order to subdue and transfer the inmate from
> the segregation to the isolation unit.' I wrote what I was told to
> write but informed the captain that, if anything of this sort would
> ever happen again, my report would read that unnecessary
> violence had taken place. I was never called on another job such
> as this, nor do I know whether it has ever occurred since then.

A new employee in a mental hospital recalled the following
experience:

> The patients have breakfast at 7:45 A.M. After breakfast, they
> had nothing to do. We had to drag some of these patients out
> of bed, and I thought it was cruel. But, when I did try to talk
> to the supervisor about this, she said that these patients must
> be treated as normal people. It was generally ignored that even

normal people would like to sleep late on days when they had nothing to do. A number of times, some of these patients would be hard to wake up in the morning, and they would lose their privileges. Later on, while working on the afternoon shift, I found out the reason why some of these patients were hard to wake up. They were being given more sedatives than prescribed by the afternoon shift. It was a habit among the afternoon shift to keep patients out of their hair by overdosing them with sedatives.

You're probably thinking, "Why isn't something done?" "How could workers who are supposed to be professionals allow these things to happen and not try to correct them?" "Why don't I publicly expose the people involved?" A young psychologist related the following experience:

While working at a state hospital for the mentally retarded, I noticed a young man who did not appear retarded. After reviewing his past history and current test results, it appeared that he simply never had the opportunity for any sort of formal education. His initial admission was due to a physical reason and had resulted in ten years of care, but with no regard to his intellectual development. I submitted a short report stating his past and present circumstances and requested that immediate action be taken to begin his education. It was submitted through 'proper channels,' but, before anything beneficial could be done, it was turned into a press release by an overreacting employee. The press coverage was hardly flattering and served only to embarrass the resident and the institution and create several uncomfortable moments for myself.

An exposé of an isolated incident seldom results in an improvement of treatment. Incidents such as these will force you to make a moral decision. What will you do if you see clients being abused, brutalized, hurt, or damaged?

The Urge to Change the Organization

The agency or organization for which you work has norms—some of which you understand by now. Perhaps you find that you want to change some of those norms. Remember, it is a big, complex, bureaucratic organization, and it is very difficult to change even if you have all the information you need. You were probably hired because you're bright, dependable, and showed some leadership potential. These same traits can lead to your dismissal. Trading your job and a future opportunity for a chance to change the organization is a big decision. Before you make your decision, read Chapter 7.

The incidents described in the past few pages each represent a brief period in the lives of the clients. Our society tolerates these kinds of activities, largely because the clients are powerless and the abuses are private. Moreover, even when such activities are exposed, does the public believe the convict or the warden? The hospital director or the incoherent patient? Moreover, it also needs to understood that the clients involved in the incidents previously described came to their particular situations through a long series of events — e.g., the prisoner in solitary confinement is not a first offender. Thus it is difficult to make judgements or draw conclusions based on a single incident.

Things that go unnoticed and don't receive much publicity are things that we easily forget. A dripping water faucet doesn't scream out to be fixed. A teacher who puts down students (consciously or unconsciously) day after day isn't usually fired for that behavior. As long as clients are damaged slowly and intermittently, nobody seems to be disturbed. A schoolteacher, discussing the results and consequences of achievement testing, described the following incidents:

> For the English teacher, the most important score is the reading score. This score is used to place the student at a reading level of his vocabulary and comprehension. The average reading level of an incoming freshman should be 9.0 [ninth grade]. If the freshman has a 5.6 score, this means that the freshman is reading at the level of a person who is a little over halfway through the fifth grade. Likewise, an 11.0 reading level would suggest a proficiency in reading equal to a student who had almost finished the eleventh grade in high school. Two instances concerning reading scores remain etched in my mind. The first instance was slightly amusing, the second extremely unfortunate. The first instance concerned a boy in my seventh-hour class. He was alert, articulate, and intelligent, and I was unable to correlate this with his fifth-grade reading level. Although this puzzled me, I didn't have time to solve the problem, since he was quickly extricated from my class and placed in the seventh-hour reading clinic. In a few weeks he returned. In that short time, he had mastered all the reading skills and was retested by the reading teacher. His reading level was over twelfth grade. Ironically, he turned out to be the most prolific reader in the class.
>
> The second reading-score problem concerned a girl in my second-hour English class. Her test results were average. Consequently, I was surprised when she could not even come close to passing what the majority of students considered an average test. As she continued to fail the tests, I postulated that she was:

(A) boy crazy, (B) apathetic, (C) bored to death by English class, or (D) all of the above. My somewhat boggled mind finally arrived at the conclusion that she could not read properly. Unfortunately, by this time she had already failed the first semester.

All of us have been students. We have worked in elementary school classrooms for about seven thousand hours. The crowded conditions, the noise, and the long lines we all experienced would not be tolerated as working conditions by most labor unions today. Somehow, during those seven thousand hours, we learned not to be enthusiastic about learning. Remember in the first and second grade how difficult it was not to jump up, make a little noise, and wave your hand when you knew the right answer? In the fourth grade, you probably sat in your seat and put your arm straight in the air when you thought you knew the answer. If you were really excited, you might have waved your hand. If you were still responding to questions in junior high, your enthusiasm had probably reached the point at which you raised one arm and propped it up with your other arm, resting your elbow on the desk. The death of curiosity, enthusiasm, and creativity is a small, slow, constant process of erosion. Students who don't, can't, or won't make it through the educational process become probationers, dropouts, inmates, or patients in another agency of the human-service system. One frustrated social worker described the poor coordination this way:

> A caseworker with seventy cases couldn't sit down and rap with one person or do any sort of therapy and administer to their other cases. So they would try and refer this case to Mental Health, but Mental Health had no people to go out and visit their homes; they weren't functioning in that way. They were dealing strictly in medical ways with a lot of the cases. So the caseworker tried to find other resources to compensate for Mental Health. They would try to put the children [in foster homes]; they would try to set up a homemaker with the family so that the mother wouldn't go completely crazy; they would try to get the children in a summer camp. The case became more and more complex, more and more diffuse, more degenerative as the basic crux of the problem was not sufficiently met. So these cases just became fantastically complex sagas.

Organizations and institutions such as jails, clinics, schools, and hospitals have the money they need to hire you. They are the places and the agencies that the community uses to help people grow, learn, or change in some way. The incidents that were described earlier in this chapter may seem to support the notion that these organizations are "human warehouses" rather than places in which people receive help. Incidents such as those can cause a new employee to decide that it's time for revolution. Not all staff members are cruel, incompetent, and indifferent. Not all institutions and agencies are demoralizing. There is cause for optimism. A mental-health technician describes the changes she has seen within ten years:

> People were sitting on benches along the walls of the cottage, one after the other. Very many were elderly. There were no comforts that I would think an old person there had the right to expect. The ward was dark and drab, with two or three aides and perhaps a nurse on duty. The patient population was over one hundred. The dorms were locked during the day, and no one could lie down. The floors were bare. Two days a week they had bath day. I don't know if that means they had two baths a week or they divided patients into two groups and had one bath a week — probably the latter. Patients lined up stripped naked, waiting in line for baths.
>
> Well, this is a thing of the past. The hospital now is to be used as a treatment center for the acutely mentally ill. Much of the housing has been remodeled and air conditioned. Some is quite modern. [As they improve] patients are free to come and go as they please without being stopped by a locked door. Treatment plans are written up when a patient enters the hospital and followed up until the patient is released. Some are even obtaining jobs on the outside and remain at hospitals several weeks until they get used to their new environment and can take the strain of living on the outside.

At another institution, a therapist reports the following:

> Less than five years ago, the mentally handicapped residents were living twenty-five to a ward, which consisted of one huge room with beds and a bathroom. They were locked in this room all day, except for meals. Because of staff shortage, no one could even attempt to teach the residents basic self-help skills. The daily routine closely resembled an assembly line.
>
> Today, through efforts of the legislators and dedicated administrators, these same residents are living eight to a cottage; not a single room, but a fully equipped home with seven rooms, including kitchen and laundry facilities. Adequate staff is present, and the residents are receiving the training needed in developing self-help skills. They are finally getting the opportunity to become the individuals they are.

A girls' basketball coach in a large inner-city school who had seen too many girls get pregnant and drop out of school decided to do something:

It took two years, but we finally got a ten-bed baby care facility right here in school. It took a lot of doing to get all of those agencies to work together. Last year I believe ten of these young mothers stayed in school because of that. It was a picture that the younger girls will never forget — seeing these mothers at lunch time and any other time they had, taking care of their babies. At the same time, I was working with the men's coaches. They had slogans like 'be a real man . . . don't make a baby if you can't be a father.' You know, this year only half of those baby cribs were used by students. I can't be sure, but I think the picture these young mothers and fathers showed to the rest of the school has made a difference.

The Important People

The trend is clear. Clients are finally becoming important in most human-service organizations. The trend may be a new phase or an organizational revolution. Clients are served as human persons. Agencies and institutions are being judged in humanitarian ways. On the other hand, purely economic and administrative values have not been thrown out; they are being tempered by an emphasis on services to people.

Some organizations are beginning to respond to their clients' human needs. A few social-casework agencies are even talking about street-therapy programs. Reform schools are beginning to provide real educational opportunities and skill training that is not related to organizational maintenance. Observers have noted that in the past, most institutional training programs were related to institutional maintenance. A security institution for boys offered welding, cooking, barbering, and electrical and carpentry apprenticeships for honor boys. These trades were needed to secure and maintain the institution. Rural institutions used to offer agriculturally related training. Until the late 1960s, dairy herds were maintained in many state correctional and mental hospital facilities.

Clients' Rights

Consumerism is beginning to affect human-service organizations. The client is beginning to influence the agency. For years, we have had token advisory boards, student councils, and so on, but the present trend seems to be real. Recent court decisions have determined that mental patients have the right to be treated, and that students have the right to be educated. In other words, clients have the right to receive service. Schwitzgebel (1976:817) suggests that contracts be written for service that describe the process and expected outcome of treatment and specify that a portion of the fee is contingent on the success of the treatment.

The increase in clients' decision-making power is largely a result of the 1970s trends in human rights and civil rights activities. Social movements affecting blacks, women, native Americans, welfare recipients, gays, and children's rights are examples of these activities. Changes in attitudes and laws regarding clients' rights have challenged the traditional paternalism of many large institutions. Many medical and psychiatric facilities post a Client's Bill of Rights to emphasize the rights that staff and others may forget or ignore. These usually include a right to treatment or to refuse treatment, and rights to privacy, safety, comfort, and others appropriate for the setting.

It seems reasonable for us to support legislation that would stop drug research on prisoners. Massachusetts tried to pass such a law, only to have five hundred inmates sign a petition against the bill. One prisoner testified against the measure. The inmates wanted the opportunity to do something interesting and socially worthwhile! The bill was consequently defeated (Schwitzgebel 1976:818).

Many institutions and agencies are beginning to see clients as a scarce resource. More programs and services are being developed to retain clients, to satisfy needs that the clients did not originally bring to the organization, and to recruit new clients. An example of this practice can be found in higher education. Many colleges and universities are offering credit for life experiences, courses developed by students, close-to-home residence centers, and concentrated weekend classes.

As the demand for accountability becomes more important, clients can play a key role. Even though the effectiveness of human-service programs is difficult to evaluate in standard ways, you will be expected to demonstrate the effectiveness of your program. One method to evaluate how a program is doing is to ask clients during a process known as *focus groups*. Such groups usually consist of a small number—usually less than twelve—of clients who are carefully selected for their representativeness. A comfortable atmosphere is created for them to meet and freely respond to a previously announced set of questions and issues. These focus groups are typically led by a fellow professional who has had contact with similar clients and is skillful at encouraging discussion, soliciting alternative opinions, and communicating respect and value for the ideas of the participants. As a new staff member, you are likely not to be chosen to lead such a group, but the opportunity to be a quiet participant could be an excellent learning experience. The comments and observations of these groups are carefully recorded and used as one set of information to look at program effectiveness, devise new programming ideas, and to obtain some assessment of the overall quality of the organization's services. Clients are also most important when an organization is forced to justify its existence on a solely economic basis. For example, the extended placement of a foster child as opposed to the disruption of that placement followed by a series of new foster homes may be worth thousands of dollars more than the intensive services provided to the current foster parents.

Another example of client value is in the corporate world. As profits decline, corporate-sponsored child care may become one of the targets for cost reduction. As a staff member in such a child care program, you will need client support for internal political reasons, but you will also need an economic justification. Such justification is difficult to produce. Reduced absences and improved production do not appear to be important variables. However, it is clear that reduced staff turnover can be one positive result of corporate-sponsored child care. It is estimated that the cost of replacing one middle-level professional is at least $25,000. It would not take many of these individual cases to justify the expense for a child care center (Friedman, 1991). As a new employee, it is not likely that you will be responsible for producing such information; but again, the opportunity to participate in such an evaluation could be a rich learning experience.

Former Clients as Staff Members

Today, many former clients are becoming staff members; some people see this as a very positive trend. (On the other hand, teachers were former students, and this has done little to change public education.) Drug-treatment programs staffed, and even run, by former addicts, probation officers who were once wards of the court, and handicapped rehabilitation counselors are part of this trend. These staff members bring a different understanding to the job and are helpful, because they are able to see the client's world as the client sees it. A word of caution: the typical student does not become a teacher. The typical drug addict does not become a counselor. These are unusual former clients. They are most likely the ones who "bought in," the ones who were conforming clients. Although former clients may have a unique perspective, we can't assume that they speak for all clients. A social caseworker described one former client/staff member in the following way:

Joan was a super con artist. She'd look like she was really working her ass off when she was not doing anything, and acting as if she really knew what was going on when she didn't. She was a very intelligent lady, but she was so insecure. She didn't realize that people would accept her for who she was. She had pulled herself up, and her attitude was 'If I can do it, why can't they?' So she was punitive to clients. She'd see a mother beating a child and figure that this is a bad mother. She couldn't see that maybe the mother was frustrated and angry with a lot of other things and taking it out on the child. Joan didn't want to work with the mother. Joan and I butted heads over a lot of these kinds of issues, but she taught me a lot about the streets, and for that I'm grateful.

Each client and staff member enters the system in his or her own way. Your clients have histories. You may want to find out about them and consider spending your efforts in getting them out of the system.

Summary

Clients, students, inmates, or wards are the reason for your job as a human-service worker. You and the clients make the organization run. It's likely that the clients are more experienced in their role than you are in your job. Remember what you and your schoolmates did to the substitute teachers? You may have known more about being a student than they knew about being a teacher. The treatment you receive from clients may resemble this at first. But as you become more familiar with the organization and more comfortable with your role, you'll be in a better position to establish positive relationships with clients.

Some staff members may appear to be indifferent, incompetent, or even cruel. The thrill of your new job may fade into "What am I doing here?" At this point, a personal journal may help you to keep a balanced perspective.

Discussion Questions

1. In what ways did you test your teachers' limits in junior and senior high school? What methods did your classmates use?
2. What traits do you dislike most in other people? Which of these traits do you have?
3. What do you feel when somebody you are trying to help uses you? When did that happen last? What did you do?

4. Is it a part of your job to change the personal values of clients? What values should they have?

References

Bernstein, G. S., and Halaszyn, J.A. 1989. *Human Services? . . . That Must Be so Rewarding*. Baltimore: Paul H. Brookes Publishing Co.

Braswell, M., Fletcher, T., and Miller, L. 1990. *Human Relations and Corrections*. Prospect Heights: Waveland Press, Inc.

Friedman, D.E. 1991. *Linking Work—Family Issues to the Bottom Line*. The Conference Board, New York.

Jacobs, J. B. 1974. *The Making of a Correctional Officer 1974*. Unpublished mimeograph, Illinois Department of Corrections.

Jacobs, J. B., and Retsky, H. G. 1975. Prison guard. *Urban Life*, 4(1).

Jourard, S. 1964. *The Transparent Self*. Princeton, NJ: Van Nostrand.

Licata, J. W., and Willower, D. J. 1975. Student brinkmanship and the school as a social system. *Educational Administration Quarterly*, 9(2), 1-14.

Maslow, A. H. 1962. *Toward a Psychology of Being*. New York: Van Nostrand Reinhold.

May, R. 1950. *The Meaning of Anxiety*. New York: The Ronald Press Co.

O'Banion, T., and O'Connell, A. 1970. *The Shared Journey*. Englewood Cliffs, NJ: Prentice Hall.

Schwitzgebel, R. K. 1976. A contractual model for the protection of the rights of institutionalized mental patients. *American Psychologist*, 30(8), 815-20.

Smith, L. M., and Geoffrey, W. 1968. *The Complexities of an Urban Classroom: An Analysis toward a General Theory of Teaching*. New York: Holt, Rinehart and Winston.

Toffler, A. 1970. *Future Shock*. New York: Random House.

3 The Organization

Modern society has become so complex and its people so transient that neighbor helping neighbor is simply not enough. Few traditional communities remain. When our older relatives become feeble, some of us are able to take care of them in our own homes. More likely, they will be cared for in convalescent, nursing, and shelter-care homes. Some forms of helping have become profit-making businesses; serious abuses are common, and many are made public.

It's easy to criticize the way in which our society has organized the delivery of help. Bureaucratic organization has weaknesses, and it is the subject of much ridicule. No one has come up with a good substitute for bureaucracy as a means of organizing a group of people and, at the same time, checking on workers to see that they are doing what they're supposed to do. Many of the bureaucratic weaknesses detailed in this book and many others may not be caused by the structure, but rather by the people who operate it.

Institutions and organizations have a life of their own. They stagnate. They reorganize. They breed. They seem to be fed by idealism and cynicism. They are staffed by idiots and geniuses. They are governed by commissions, trustees, and boards. These governing bodies are dominated by people who have become well known (or at least visible) through channels of business, finance, and law — people who probably view agencies and institutions in terms of debits and credits. Mandell (1975) discusses the characteristics of board members in the following paragraphs:

When one examines the background of members of the board of directors of a major hospital, college, or United Fund drive, one finds that most of them own property (business executives), serve those who own property (lawyers and political officials), or earn large salaries in a profession (doctors). Occasionally a union leader sits on a board, but hardly ever an assembly line worker or a waitress.

One could argue that this should make little difference to the actual work of an agency, which is carried out by professionals. Yet the administrator of an agency carries the board's wishes to the workers. Agency administrators may make some policy contrary to the wishes of some board members, but the board will have to be convinced of the wisdom of it before the policy is funded. I am sure there are some agencies in which the professionals are more conservative than the board. Professionals have their own jobs and agency and professional culture to protect.

The Victorian philanthropists could not envision working with the poor as equals. With precious few exceptions, twentieth-century human-service workers and their boards of directors are no different. Top-down elitism still prevails over bottom-up democracy. However, during the 1960s, people challenged the hegemony of elitists in the social services, and once the people have tasted power, the battle has been joined (Mandell, 1975:65).

Genuinely community-based programs are emerging. A growing body of research supports both the effectiveness and efficiency of locally controlled human-service programs (Hegar and Hunzeker, 1988; Golden, 1990). The resignation of the United Way chief executive in 1992, after disclosures of a rather exorbitant lifestyle, not only supported the move toward local control but also highlighted the responsibility for accountability in not-for-profit board members.

Philanthropy may be the very glue that keeps capitalism from falling apart at the seams. The economist Kenneth Boulding believes that "nonexchange" transfers of funds, such as foundation grants, are essential to the survival of American capitalism. . . . In other words, if there were no charity to mask the gross inequalities of income and wealth, people might catch on to what is happening and get angry enough to change it (Mandell, 1975:66). A more positive view is presented by Peter Drucker (1991) when he claims that virtually every success in solving social problems has been achieved by non-governmental, non-profit organizations. Some 900,000 non-profit organizations exist "employing" 90 million volunteers. A select few of these volunteers are members of governing boards.

The Board

During their meetings, board members spend a great deal of time discussing budgets. After they've approved routine items, such as the payment of outstanding bills, they begin to discuss other numbers. Maxwell (1973) has labeled this phenomenon "number numbness." Board members don't deal with staff members or clients; they deal with numbers that they can count. Numbers about daily population, average daily attendance, numbers of placements, rates of pledge payments, numbers of runaways, and numbers of credit hours produced are of great concern to board members. Comparisons are made between current numbers and those of a month or a year ago. Any obvious differences between current figures and figures from past records cause board members to ask for an explanation. The superintendent or executive director is always ready with an answer — usually one that has three parts. (For some reason, a three-part answer always seems to be more impressive.) The board then proceeds to count more numbers; however, these are related to employees, raises, new hires, retirees, the ratio of staff members to clients, and staff production rates. This is followed by a calculation of operating costs for organizational maintenance. Numbers of vehicles, beds, desks, rooms, meals, miles, clothes, uniforms, balls, guns, and enema bags are topics of discussion. Such concerns may seem unimportant to you; however, careful accounting, which requires counting, is needed to maintain a cash flow and pay staff members.

University budgets are based in large part on numbers of students and numbers of credit hours earned. Many states compute university and college budgets based on credit hours earned, thereby giving greater weight to those hours as students progress from their first year to graduate school.

One rural mental-health worker put it this way:

> The monthly client-contact report is what keeps the agency going. My report is added in with the other workers', and that is partly how the regional board decides how much money we get. The reports seemed like a pain to fill out. When I first started here, I used to take them lightly and didn't even keep good track of the number of hours I spent. One day, my supervisor told me that the budget was going to be cut, because the other satellite offices had been increasing their contact with clients. We had stayed about the same. It was then I realized the importance of these reports.

The associate director of an urban mental-service-delivery agency has a "hell of a time" convincing the staff that statistical reports are important:

> I used to talk myself blue in the face to the teachers and social workers in the alternative school about these reports. We have a policy that, every time a kid is absent, someone goes to visit their home — to check on them, but mostly to provide tutoring and counseling. It also provides contact with the parents or guardian. Anyhow, I don't know how many times I had told them to report these visits, but they usually didn't. Our school district reimbursement depends upon the average daily attendance. These home visits count toward a part of the average daily attendance. A few months back, we had a real budget crunch, and I was forced to give two teachers notice based upon a declining school district reimbursement.
>
> Since the notices to these teachers, the teachers and social workers have been reporting not just the kids in school but those they go to visit — even if they're in detention. This has made what looks like a 15 percent increase in our average daily attendance. Now, I've got to check to see if they are fudging a little on these reports.

Simply put, all boards are responsible to somebody — the state legislature, the church, the immediate community, the taxpayer, or the public — and they are held accountable to those people. In their effort to do a good job, all boards need to count numbers so they can judge what is going on in the organization. After the debit/credit needs of the board are satisfied, items dealing with client services are discussed.

It's difficult to evaluate the components of a program by counting. The number of foster home replacements may have little to do with the quality of life for a youthful client. The average daily attendance in school may not be related to what students are learning. Smaller caseloads for probation officers or smaller classes for teachers have not been shown to produce better client results. Crime rates go up when the number of police officers is increased, simply because more arrests are made. In other words, people-changing programs are very difficult to evaluate.[1] The board needs to ask questions such as "Does your organization really do any good for people?" or "What has your organization accomplished lately?". These questions are difficult to answer. Most organizations count people in their attempt to answer. People are counted in case reports, incident write-ups,

---

[1] Two of the most useful books written on this subject are *Evaluation of Human Service Programs*, edited by Attkisson et al., (Academic Press, 1978) and *Qualitative Evaluation and Research Methods* by Patton (Sage, 1990).

community placements, and referrals. Most board members lack the time and the skill needed to perform a meaningful evaluation of any human-service organization. One of the major tasks of the top professionals in any organization is to apply complex evaluation designs to a specific organization. Effective administrators report the results of such assessments to board members.

My experience as a member of two boards was both rewarding and frustrating. Board members have good intentions. They usually serve without pay, take time from their jobs and families, and vote honestly. Most of their mistakes can be traced to two facts: (1) most program questions have no right answers, and (2) boards can act only on the basis of available information. They must depend on their professional staff to supply most of that information. It is a fortunate board that has professional staff who provide alternatives based on accurate and understandable information.

All commissions, or boards, include staff members who keep the board informed so that no decisions are made that would damage the reputation of the organization. These individuals must be experts in keeping others calm. Continued budget support depends on smooth operations; therefore, organizational changes are potentially damaging. Some people interpret such changes to mean that the governing body and the staff have not been doing the best in the past. Changes are risky, because new ideas that have not been tested may not work well. Many changes create work for staff members. If changes are to be accepted by the public, that public will require education—a tough job that is often neglected. The picture at the top is that of a governing body of uninformed individuals with a "staff" who want to keep things on an even keel. This is the status quo.

The director of your organization or agency reports to the governing body, perhaps through somebody else. As long as your director runs a tight and quiet ship, the board remains satisfied. This kind of arrangement makes it very difficult to change the way in which an organization does business. The final section in this chapter introduces some strategies for change.

Some Administrative Types

Every bureaucratic organization has administrators and administrators and administrators. We have come to relate administration with leadership. Many administrators have studied the best means of getting people to do their jobs and know how to keep an organization running smoothly. Administrators themselves have also been studied. A brief description of some of those studies is included in order to give you a general idea of this literature. Most of these authors begin by dividing administrators into two categories and then discussing the ways in which these two types of administrators behave.

Etzioni (1965) describes two major administrative types: instrumental and expressive. The instrumental leader needs overt respect, deals well with hostility, and worries about the budget and how it is distributed. Etzioni contrasts this with the expressive leader, who needs to be loved and to be friendly. The expressive leader is less able to stand hostility than the instrumental leader and has the need to maintain a close relationship with people in various parts of the system. Etzioni's work has been followed by refinements of the terms "instrumental" and "expressive." In *The Human Side of Enterprise*, MacGregor (1960) uses relatively analogous terms — *theory X* (instrumental) and *theory Y* (expressive). Blake and Mouton's *Corporate Excellence through Grid Organization Development* (1968) is based on two extremes of leadership styles: concern for production (instrumental) and concern for people (expressive). Hersey and Blanchard (1988) describe a situational leadership model in which the leader shows relationship behavior (expressive), task behavior (instrumental), or a combination of the two.

Additional detail for each administrative type is developed by these authors, dealing with concepts of power, control, authority, subordinate/superordinate relationships, communications, and human relations. An analysis of this additional information is beyond the scope of this book. However, the concepts of organizational change and conflict management are discussed in some detail later in this chapter. Of more immediate interest are the administrative types commonly found in human-service organizations.

One professional helper describes her supervisor as "just the nicest, most religious, most rigid, most frightened, most old, most mileage-oriented person I've ever met, who cares very much that the papers have to be made out just right." What type of supervisor, manager, or boss do you have? Several types of leaders' characteristics are described in the following paragraphs. Some of these characteristics and traits may be found in all of us, but they seem especially easy to see in administrators.

Cut and Cover. Country folks know what a sickle bar is and how it works. A sickle bar is a hay and grass mower that sticks out close to the ground from the side of a machine. It has a series of fixed blades on a bar that moves back and forth against a set of teeth that do not move. If all of the blades are sharp and none of the teeth are broken, all of the grass is cut by the back and forth motion of the blades against the teeth. The hay falls into a neat pattern in the field. Even if some of the teeth are broken or some of the blades are dull, the hay that is cut pushes over the uncut hay—the appearance of the field is no different than when the hay is properly mowed. Some supervisors cut and cover. The operator of the defective mower isn't found out until it is time to rake and bale the hay. The nursing supervisor isn't found out until the body of the "runaway" patient is found on the floor by his bed.

Please Mommy or Daddy? It is human to want to be liked. Some administrators, bosses, and supervisors behave as if people work harder for somebody they like; a supervisor/staff relationship should be based on more than that. Respect should be based on performance on the part of both the staff and the supervisor. Many adults are still dependent—they need a parent figure. Some administrators take advantage of this need, and some even go as far as to deliberately hire and keep a staff of the dependent type. Staff lunches, coffee hours, and drinks after work often resemble a family gathering with father at the head of the table, rather than a relaxed work group. This variation of the expressive leadership style is common in "socializing" organizations, such as schools, churches, and rehabilitation centers. Berliner, who worked in the federal penitentiary in Fort Worth, saw many kinds of administrators in his bureaucracy. He said that the fallacy of this type of administration is the assumption that adults retain pervasive dependency attitudes and believe that the function of work is to please rather than to satisfy more mature needs (Berliner, 1971).

What Shall We Do? Democracy is becoming popular. Participative management is sometimes taken to mean that group decisions are always better than individual effort and responsibility. Even though the majority has often been wrong, there is often wisdom in numbers. Sharp administrators know when key staff people should have influence on decisions—these people have information from the firing line that administrators don't have. On the other hand, administrators sometimes have information that is unavailable to subordinates. Efficient administrators make it clear whether an opinion or a decision is expected.

Staff members who get their heads bumped too many times will rebel; the lumps come when they think that what they say really counts, only to find out that a decision has already been made. Said professionally, overparticipation in the decision-making process, as well as decisional deprivation, tends to increase staff dissatisfaction (Conway, 1976).

I Really Don't Like This Job. A friend of mine campaigned vigorously to be elected as the chairperson of an academic department in a university. Within two weeks after taking office, he began to draw Xs through the dates on a calendar in order to keep track of the number of days he had left in his term as chairperson. Often, these Xs were drawn before an audience. He made comments such as "I can't wait to get back to my full-time teaching." Some people apologize for being administrators by saying things such as "Somebody has to do the paper work." They are very uncomfortable when they have to tell people "no" or "We don't have any money for that." There are probably many reasons for this attitude, but it seems that, in the helping professions, there is a widely held belief that the only people who really make contributions are those who are in a direct-treatment role. It has become very popular to attack and criticize bureaucratic managers and administrators. It is difficult when frontline people who have participated in these attacks on administrators to suddenly find themselves one of "the enemy." Therefore, they need to apologize for their administrative position.

The Super Helper. Some administrators treat staff members as clients. Staff members get the feeling that they are being treated, educated, rehabilitated, or counseled. This kind of administrator seems to enjoy helping staff out of predicaments. Extreme cases of this type enjoy taking care of and doing things for the staff. They seem to imply that what they normally would be expected to do for the staff in the course of their position is instead a special favor.

You, My Staff. These administrators act as if staff people were working for them. They see staff members as extra arms and legs to do their bidding. Of course, you work under the guidance and direction of your supervisors. They can have you fired, even though they don't pay you — staff members and administrators are paid by the same people. Both groups should be working for clients and delivering services.

The Admiral. Clean, neat, spotless, scrubbed, and tidy are the watchwords. The appearance must be "shipshape." The desk and office of this administrator are always uncluttered. Pride is taken in the massive, cross-referenced index files and in their personal appearance. They consume a lot of paper. You will be impressed by their concern for your grooming and clothes.

Mr. Peter Principle. These administrators can be either male or female. They are fearful, shy, and indecisive. Many of them have been promoted without the needed education and training to perform at a higher level in the organization. From their humble beginnings, they have risen to the level of incompetence—and it shows (Hersey and Blanchard, 1989).

The Party Line. These administrators are seen most often in the largest organizations. You never get to know what they believe. All that is told you has come from "upstairs." If the staff members read and had copies of memos and orders, they wouldn't need these administrators; they direct when they are told to direct, they supervise on schedule, and they evaluate on the appropriate forms.

The Boss's Job

I do not know anybody who is an ideal boss. The qualities we expect of human-service administrators probably cannot be found in one person. In order to be effective, an administrator needs skills in human relations, decision making, personnel practices, budget management, project evaluation, program management, and planning. Those who come the closest to having all these skills would likely be paid much more in private industry than they would in the management of human services.

Administrators are expected to know something about the actual service an organization is supposed to provide. Moreover, staff members expect them to know about their jobs and understand the daily frustrations they experience. Don't be surprised if your superiors seem to have a lot of other things on their minds—they do. As human-service organizations expand, the pressure on the system increases, and the need for coordination and planning becomes greater. However, as the workload goes up and the budget goes down, planning and coordination are the first things to suffer. Your organization's budget is made for one or two years at a time and the organization's achievements are considered when funds are provided. Planning and coordination do not show results in one or even two years; therefore, few organizations risk part of their budget for long-term planning. Constant financial concerns may be one of the distractions that keep administrators from being more understanding of and interested in staff problems. As the federal government becomes the source of more and more funding, administrators need to keep track of the new agencies, names, laws, and bureaus that control the money. Much of an administrator's time can be spent writing grant applications and proposals to compete for funds.

Assistants

Assistants are important people; they're usually in charge of many areas that can make a big difference in your job. An assistant's responsibilities include ordering supplies, supervising vacation schedules, overtime pay, work records, special time off, and minor changes in routine operations. On the surface, these functions may not seem to be very important, but do not be deceived. The informal power of these assistants can be great. Some of them have worked themselves into positions from which they are able to dispense political favors. If they like you, supplies will come quickly, you will have the vacations you prefer, your promotion papers will be forwarded promptly without important documents being misplaced, and personal leave will be approved.

Administrators value their assistants and ask them for a good deal of advice on decisions that relate to their area of responsibility. In human-service organizations, these assistants are usually what Etzioni would call instrumental types. They focus their concerns on the supply, demand, and allocation of resources to the organization. Often, these assistants act as buffers and take the heat off the boss — they are the administrators who tell you "no." Instrumental assistants are likely to make their bosses look good. With assistants of the instrumental type, the big boss may be mistakenly viewed as more accommodating and less able to withstand conflict than is really the case. The boss may appear to be an expressive leader who is concerned about the social and emotional needs of the staff. Be careful. It has been my experience that administrative assistants reflect the attitudes and values of their superiors.

Administrative assistants may seem evasive when you ask them questions. Remember, they aren't the boss, and they don't make decisions openly for which the boss would be responsible later. They may be evasive in their answers, even though they know what the boss plans to do or what the boss would approve of if he or she were asked in the right way. Assistants' formal responsibility is usually very limited, but often their informal power is great. They occupy a key link in the chain of command.

Your Immediate Supervisor

The link in the chain of command who is closest to you, your supervisor, may have a lot to do with your present job satisfaction and your future career. Take a very close look at your supervisor. You may see your immediate supervisor as a boss. Be aware that the department chairpersons, the ward supervisors, the charge nurses, the team leaders, the lieutenants, or whatever they may be called in your organization, are also subordinates — they themselves have many bosses. In fact, they are on the lowest rung of administration in your organization, and they may view themselves as powerless, helpless pawns who are constantly being used by the organization. On the other hand, your supervisor may feel like the most important member of the team. Obviously, your supervisor's feelings about the job will have a great influence on what is thought of you and how you are treated.

Supervisors who have recently graduated from specialized college training may feel important, but they may lack experience. Most of their knowledge may have been derived from books and lectures. Give them a chance. You expect them to treat you with an open mind, so the least you can do is treat them in the same way. It's more likely that your supervisors have had the job you have now or one very much like it. They have probably worked in the organization for a few years and have seen people like you come and go (and probably long enough to see people above them succeed and fail).

If your supervisors have been where you are, they may feel they know very clearly how you should do your job. The way in which they see your job now is determined by the way in which they saw the job when they had it. In other words, their perception of your role is based on their personal experience. Your perception of the job will differ from theirs. As a new employee, you would probably be wise to accept the supervisor's view of your job, even though it may differ from your own view or the view that was presented by the people who hired you. Sometimes it's helpful to put yourself in the supervisor's role. What would you do? How would you act toward a new employee? Maybe your decisions would be similar to those of the supervisor. Reserve judgment until you have all the information available.

After you begin your new job, you should find out which supervisors used to have jobs similar to yours and whether they like to be asked for advice or whether they expect you to leave them alone until you're in trouble. Moreover, you need to know which institutional rules and policies each supervisor openly supports, ignores, or would like to see changed. Another helpful characteristic for you to identify is the supervisor's tolerance for conflict. Is conflict avoided, or is it viewed as an exciting potential for change?

If your supervisor has been with the organization for a long time, he or she probably has valuable information about the organization that could be of help to you. However, if you develop a poor relationship with your supervisor, they may not share this information with you when you need it. You may find yourself making mistakes that a timely piece of advice could have prevented. This will be especially true if, for some reason, you are seen as one of those new employees who won't be there too long anyway. In some human-service organizations, the staff turnover is so great that supervisors have good reason to believe you'll be gone soon. An extreme example of turnover was illustrated by the loss of three hundred prison guards in one year at a state prison that employs less than that number at any one time (Jacobs, 1975).

Never communicate to your supervisors that you think you know more about your job (or theirs) than they do. Your tone of voice, choice of words, and posture all communicate a variety of messages. You and a supervisor may say "Good morning" to each other while conveying a number of messages. One "Good morning" may indicate supplication, awareness of subordinate status, or anxiety; another may convey condescension, awareness of power, rejection, or hostility.

You communicate by means of your behavior as well as your words. Most of us aren't aware of the extent to which our pattern of behavior is coming through to other people. Look carefully at the communication pattern you use with other staff members and your supervisors. Fighting with others tends to appear in several guises — in humor, in debate and argument, in semantic quibbling, and in strategy and counter-strategy. Parliamentary procedure provides a convenient structure for socialized fighting.

We all have, to some extent, the need to control and influence others. Advertising, propaganda, guidance, education, persuasion, management, and manipulation are ways of describing our efforts to control the lives of others, to get them to do something that is good for us or that we think is good for them.

Our lives are made more predictable by controls. Formal law is one form of control. When we drive on two-way streets in the United States, we predict that the cars coming toward us will be on our left side. Moreover, our lives are made predictable by a set of natural laws. Physical exhaustion is a result of inadequate rest. Social controls make our relationships with others more predictable. The more control that is present, the less risk for the participants. Those who have the power to exert social control are labeled "authorities." How much authority do you need to have over your clients?

Organizational Control

Control is of immediate concern to those who are in authority. The most powerful tool in organizational control is information — what's "going on" and how it's "going down." In other words, your supervisor needs to know when waves are being made before the splash hits. There are many levels of administration, but all administrators have several things in common. Anyone who has supervisory responsibility has a need to know how to direct and control others. Administrators aren't happy when their superiors tell them something about their unit that they didn't already know. For example, it is a bit embarrassing for a prison guard to be told by a lieutenant that contraband has been discovered on the guard's cell block, or for a charge nurse to be told by the nursing supervisor that one of her patients has died.

In addition to control through information, each organization has its own ways and means of control. You know about some extreme physical controls that are enforced in mental hospitals and prisons. All of us were physically and emotionally controlled as children at home and as clients in school. When young children fall and skin their knees, an adult comes and says, "Don't cry." Translated, this is a directive to control feelings and behavior. In the view of one young teacher, "Control seems to have become the end rather than the means of good education. To my administrator, control is synonymous with good teaching. The job of the teacher seems to be defined as getting the new recruits to act submissive and to accept control." This young teacher's view is supported by the professional literature. Furst (1975:8) says, "School, it seems, is primarily a custodial operation," and Willower (1975:219) has made a career of studying pupil control in schools; he concludes that "client control is of paramount concern."

Those who are in authority, who have power to control the key staff, expect you to control your clients. You are on the bottom rung of the formal power ladder in your organization; try to imagine how clients must feel. Who do they control? Whom can they help? Who needs them? What would happen if you gave clients the chance to help somebody who really needs them? I tried to answer this question by giving some delinquent boys a chance to work with geriatric mental patients. The boys, who were locked up in a correctional institution, were on the bottom rung of the power and control ladder, and the mental patients were in the same position. Some of the results were dramatic. Three boys voluntarily extended their commitment to continue working with the patients. Even the delinquent boys saw a need for control in the hospital. "Two patients got into a fight on the ward. The [delinquent] jumped up and immediately separated them. He put his arm around one and talked to her quietly until she calmed down. He then sat down on the couch with one of them on each side of him and talked to both women" (Russo, 1974:532). Control doesn't have to be oppressive or brutal; this young man showed kindness and tenderness, affirming that control can be positive.

The Carnegie Corporation supported research at the University of Michigan Institute for Social Research. Studying large-scale organizations, Marcus and Cafagna (1969:127), concluded that "Whether the criterion of a good organization is that of productivity or the intelligent utilization of human resources, the findings indicate that with greater total control there is a greater sharing in control at all levels, morale is higher, consensus regarding work is greater, and organizational effectiveness is facilitated."

Control in organizations can take the form of "follow the rules" or "do it by the book and go by the schedule." I have known school principals who proudly display their master class schedule on the wall in their offices and announce that they can tell you what part of the subject is being taught right now by Ms. Smith in seventh-grade English. If you act as if you don't believe them, an intercom switch to Ms. Smith's room is turned on. Most prisons and jails are operated like this; those that are modern are equipped with video camera equipment. It becomes especially important to "go by the book" when your organization is about to be inspected, accredited, or visited by outsiders. More about this is mentioned in the next section.

Organizational Reorganization

Those who administer bureaucratic help-giving organizations use a number of reasons to explain frequent reorganization. Recently, a popular reason was efficiency; today, efficiency is rapidly being replaced by accountability. Whatever the reason for trying to reorganize, there are usually at least two truths: (1) the most recent reorganization began before the preceding one was complete, and (2) the real reason for all the fuss is to increase control—of clients, staff, money, and organizational norms.

The roles of key staff members don't change as a result of reorganization. They continue to deliver services to clients. They still have a supervisor. They continue to write reports, go to meetings, and have too much to do. Their salary doesn't change. Despite these things, reorganization can be important to staff members. Be attuned to them. Draw them on a chart. Know who your supervisors are and how many supervisors you have.

The formal organization, or the chain of command, is a part of bureaucratic organizations. In Chapter 4, we will see what happens when this chain of command is not followed. The chain of command becomes especially important when things are not going smoothly. One new teacher, who tried to help a student make a schedule change, described the following blunder:

> It was the beginning of the year, and I had this Novels class. The students must be able to read at a junior level, and it's more or less C or above kids. I had one boy in there who hated to read and was a poor reader, so I said, 'I'm going to help get you out of here, because I don't want to flunk you. You could do better on a different level.' He said, 'Okay. Fine. That's all right with me.' And I said, 'Okay, I'll tell you what to do. You go down and you talk to Ms. Adams and I will write a note about how I feel about this.' So he came back and he said, 'Ms. Adams said that I can get out, but I have to have a note from you assuring the okay.' So I wrote one. Within 20 minutes, I received a note from Ms. Adams that said, 'Report to the auditorium immediately.' They were making changes, and all the administrators and counselors were there making program changes, and the kids were lined up. She pulled me back and said, 'How dare you make a change? I am the only one who makes a change in this program!' I kept trying to explain that the kid told me she gave the okay. I couldn't even get it in until she had got her anger out. And then I told her, 'But this is just a mistake. The student told me that you had given the okay.' So it was just, you know, a misjudgment there, and I was embarrassed—almost to tears.

The response of the department chairperson seems excessive, but students must be kept track of and class size must be controlled. All institutions are responsible for knowing where their clients are at all times. The chain of command includes the flow of this information. Sign-out sheets, roll call, bed checks, and "the count" are all attempts to keep track of clients. The person who is in charge of attendance or the count is usually an assistant principal, an assistant warden, or an administrative assistant.

The Shadow Organization

In addition to the formal organization represented by neatly drawn charts, an informal organization exists in every work environment. An understanding of the informal organization is critical to your survival as a staff member. The shadow organization is the *real* organization. Groups of people who work together develop relationships, understandings, and unwritten rules; these relationships produce the shadow organization. Much of this book deals with the significant influence that individual staff members can have on the work environment.

Most of us seek support and need to know that others respect us, love us, and accept us. Some people try to keep others at a comfortable distance (withdrawal); others seek to maintain intimacy with a wide variety of people.

Few of us are as accepting of people as we might be. Liking people is not necessarily equivalent to accepting them, and vice versa. When we accept another person, we recognize that person as a human being who has strong needs and feelings, and we realize that we should listen to and understand that person so that effective relations can be established. Acceptance should be a prelude to listening. It's difficult to really listen. Most of us listen only partially to other people; consequently, we often make assumptions about their communications that are incorrect. Listening requires concentration. When we listen, we focus on other people and their communication.

Our individual needs interact with those of our coworkers to produce the shadow organization. Relationship patterns and work norms produce an influence flow and a control system. Remember, the shadow organization is not shown on a typical organizational chart. You have to make your own map or chart. One form of such a chart is called a *sociogram*—a description of social-interaction patterns among a group of people. In addition to drawing up a sociogram, you should conduct some private survey research. Ask the following questions: "In what ways do your supervisors' personal values and priorities differ from those of their supervisors', and with which superiors do they cooperate?", "Whom do they ignore, and with whom do they have trouble?", Whom do they influence, and who influences them?".

It will probably be impossible for you to obtain complete answers to all of these questions—the answers will come in pieces. Some questions will be answered sooner than others. At times, you may think you have all the pieces, only to find out, after you've gathered additional information, that your original answer was either incomplete or wrong. You can get a handle on the "influence flow" in your organization by doing a little research. Roney (1965) has developed a simple means of conducting such research. He suggests that you try to obtain answers to the following questions from each of your coworkers. Don't call a meeting and pass out questionnaires;

keep your eyes and ears open. You may even feel comfortable asking a few people directly. The four questions are:

1. From whom do you get advice and information about your job?
2. To whom do you give advice and information about their jobs?
3. From whom do you take orders?
4. To whom do you give orders?

A little counting will show you that there are eight possible combinations of answers to these questions. For instance, staff member A may feel that he takes orders from staff member B, but B doesn't think that she gives orders to A. After you've gathered some of the information (research data) you need, begin to map it. Compare it with a chart of your organization's formal structure. You may discover that the formal organization chart bears little resemblance to the way in which decisions are actually made. For instance, many organizations are moving toward a system of merit pay raises; complex rating and evaluation of employees is used to determine their merit. Each supervisor's recommendations are reviewed as the merit judgments are passed up through the organization. Despite formal, detailed procedures and processes, research has shown that teachers who are closest to their supervisors get the most merit raises (Hooker, 1978). This is not to say that staff members who maintain good relationships with their supervisors don't deserve these raises; the point is that the formal rating procedures don't appear to be the most critical variable. It's how well you get along with the boss that counts, not necessarily how well you do your job.

In addition to comparing the formal system of decision making with the shadow organization, you should look at job descriptions. Job descriptions, which are similar to the organizational chart, are usually available to outsiders and new employees. The following examples illustrate the difference between the formal job descriptions and the actual duties of two administrators.

The job description of the executive director reads: "Carry out policies adopted by the Board. Provide leadership to program development. Maintain continuous and systematic evaluation of both program and staff." In fact, the executive director develops policies for the board to approve. Rather than plan programs, the executive director reacts to program suggestions from staff members, develops programs that can be funded, and phases out programs that can't be funded. The major function of the executive director is to keep the financial wolf from the door.

The business manager's formal job description may read in part:

"Has staff relationship with executive director. Supervises bookkeeper and clerk. Maintains records related to purchasing, inventory, payroll, and federal and state audit reports." As you watch business managers operate, you may see that they maintain almost daily direct contact with and collect information from each supervisor on an individual basis. Individuals who have such detailed and up-to-the-minute information can maintain powerful organizational control. After all, most of your organization's activities involve money and, therefore, the business manager.

Another area in which a large difference usually exists between the formal organization and the shadow organization is that of norms. The formal public statements describing your organization and its philosophy may sound something like this: "We intend to be the best of our kind," "We are an organization that is constantly on the lookout for better ways of doing things," "Supervisors really care about the growth and development of staff," and "Ask for help if you need it." However, as you go about your daily tasks, you may become aware of traditions and norms that do not reflect those statements. Instead, you may hear: "People around here tend to hang on to old ways of doing things, even after they have outlived their usefulness," "Staff development and in-service training are of little importance," and "Hide your problems and avoid your supervisor."

Skillful administrators keep careful track of the informal shadow organization as they use it to accomplish their goals. Your awareness of the differences between the formal organization and the informal organization will give you more control over your future as a staff member.

Summary

The new employee usually works the longest hours, has the most contact with clients, and works at the lowest pay rate. These key staff members deliver services; they are the most important staff members. They generate the data, write the reports, and deliver the services that allow an organization to survive. The entire organization "above" these key staff members exists to support the delivery of services. This chapter describes the relationship between key staff members and supervisors, administrators, and governing boards.

The organizational charts, written job descriptions, and other printed policies, rules, and regulations are part of the formal organization. The role and function of the board, the director, the assistants, and the business manager are important to the control and information needs of an organization.

The boss's assistant, or the business manager, usually plays an important role in the shadow (or informal) organization. The shadow organization runs the informal day-to-day functioning of an agency. It's the way things are really done. The identification of staff relationships, traditional understandings, and unwritten rules are critical to the survival of a new staff member.

Discussion Questions

1. Who are the board members of your institution or agency? How closely do they fit the stereotype described in this chapter?
2. How do you judge the effectiveness of what you do with clients? What are your criteria of success on your job?
3. How would you (or do you) relate to the various administrative types discussed in this chapter?
4. If you are reading this book as part of a class, describe how you would teach this class if you were in charge. What would the consequences of the changes be? If you're on the job, how would you do things differently than your supervisor does? What would the consequences of these changes be?
5. How do you typically relate to authority figures? Describe the various ways in which other people relate to authority figures.

References

Berliner, A. 1971. Some pitfalls in administrative behavior. *Social Casework*, November, 52.

Blake, R. R., and Mouton, J. S. 1968. *Corporate Excellence through Grid Organization Development*. Houston: Gulf Publishing Co.

Conway, J. A. 1976. Test of linearity between teachers' participation in decision making and their perceptions of their schools as organizations. *Administrative Science Quarterly*, March, 21.

Drucker, P. F. 1991. It profits us to strengthen nonprofits. *The Wall Street Journal*, December 19, A-14.

Etzioni, A. 1965. Dual leadership in complex organizations. *American Sociological Review*, October, 30(5).

Furst, L. G. 1975. The educational fifth column: An expanded role for teachers. *Phi Delta Kappan*, September, 57(1), 8-10.

Golden, O. 1990. Innovation in public sector human services programs: the implications of innovation by "groping along." *Journal of Policy Analysis and Management*, 9 (2), 219-48.

Hegar, R. L., and Hunzeker, J. M. 1988. *Moving toward Empowerment-Based Practice in Public Child Welfare.* National Association of Social Workers, Inc.

Hersey, P., and Blanchard, K. 1988. *Management of Organizational Behavior.* Englewood Cliffs, NJ: Prentice Hall.

Hooker, C. P. 1978. A behavior modification model for merit U. *Phi Delta Kappan,* March, 59(7), 481.

Jacobs, J. B. 1975. *The Making of a Correctional Officer.* Unpublished paper, Center for Studies in Criminal Justice, University of Chicago Law School.

MacGregor, D. 1960. *The Human Side of Enterprise.* New York: McGraw-Hill.

Mandell, B. R. (Ed.). 1975. *Welfare in America: Controlling "The Dangerous Classes."* Englewood Cliffs, NJ: Prentice-Hall.

Marcus, P. M., and Cafagna, D. 1969. Control in modern organizations. *Public Administration Review,* November, 11.

Maxwell, A. D. 1973. Number numbness. *Liberal Education,* October, 59(3), 405-16.

Roney, J., Jr. 1965. A case study of administrative structure in a health department. *Human Organization,* Winter, 24(4).

Russo, J. R. 1974. Mutually therapeutic interaction between mental patients and delinquents. *Hospital and Community Psychiatry,* August, 25(8).

Willower, D. J. 1975. Some comments on inquiries on schools and pupil control. *Teachers' College Record,* 77(2), 219-30.

4 Your Coworkers

Established staff members have grown accustomed to the status quo. The way in which they follow procedures and relate to clients and supervisors fits the norms and traditions of the organization. New staff members' training may have included an introduction to the professional norms that influence and control staff/client relationships. All staff members have been clients in help-giving organizations at some point; at least as students or medical patients. They have had an opportunity to observe the norms that operate in schools and hospitals. However, few new staff members are familiar with the specific norms that will control and influence their relationships with the organization and the established employees.

The process of staff recruitment, hiring, training, probation, supervision, and evaluation is designed to protect the status quo of the organization. Whatever form the screening process takes, it is justified as a protection of client welfare. The people who do the screening are successful in the traditional sense of the term — they have jobs, power, and a great deal of control. Hoffer (1967:102) observes that "It is not usually the successful who advocate drastic social reforms, plunge into new undertakings in business and industry, go out to tame the wilderness, or evolve new modes of expression in literature, art, music, etc." Hoffer goes further and says that the misfits in the human race try to fit in by changing the world, rather than themselves. These responsible revolutionaries are the type who were, and are, pioneers — the courageous misfits. An exaggerated example of this type is the individual who has failed

55

in mundane, everyday affairs and so reaches out for the impossible. (When people fail to do the impossible, they have much company.) Teachers see this phenomenon in nonreading elementary students who aspire to careers in biophysics or space exploration. To return to the point, the elimination of "pioneer" types is one part of the selection process that helps to maintain the status quo.

Most staff recruitment is based on lists of job seekers who have met minimum qualifications and who have achieved an above-average score on a battery of tests—even though the test results may have little relationship to eventual performance on the job. In 1975, Menges documented that "Predictive validity of the tests has not been established" (p. 201). He concluded that, even if we could define good practice and professional ethics in various fields, it seems unlikely that these would be related to test scores. Usually, those who get as far as an interview do not behave in radical ways—they want to be hired.

Probationary reviews are intended to weed out incompetents and any new staff members who are causing trouble. New employees who cause trouble are not necessarily doing so by choice. Each of us has built a number of selves to be used in various situations (Goffman, 1969). The way in which we behave with the Sunday school teacher may differ from the way in which we behave with our best friend. Our supervisors are presented with a self that differs from the self we present to our subordinates. In the life-long process of socialization, we learn various rules of conduct, values and attitudes, and desirable behaviors through which we fulfill our social obligations. These patterns of behavior become a part of us; therefore, to a large extent, we are not fully conscious of the choices we make as we enter a new social situation, such as a job. Yet, if we make the wrong choice, the mistake is immediately brought to consciousness. No support comes from others. We feel a loss of face. The wrong combinations of patterns chosen at the wrong time can produce trouble for both the new employee and the organization.

Usually, new employees who have survived probation have learned the conforming behaviors of the organization. As a result, the people who are employed by bureaucratic helping organizations often are not prepared to sacrifice their income for a principle of justice, fair play, or efficiency. These are people who are employed by an organization that has developed a satisfactory reputation over the years and an image that has allowed it to survive and perhaps flourish. When money is tight, a good solid organizational image is especially important because it ensures continued budget support. Moreover, many people are afraid to change goals and ways of doing business. You constantly hear "This is the way we have always done things around here" or "Oh, we can't do that. It's too risky."

As a new employee in a human-service organization, you may see conflicts between what ought to be and what is. Almost all of us want things to be the way we feel they ought to be — we want to improve them. We want change. You will be frustrated by the discrepancy between the services a client needs and the services you are supposed to deliver; this frustration is felt by every new employee. Many employees in your organization have tried to make changes. As you look around, it's clear that very few of them were effective in their efforts. However, some of them have been successful, and a small number of established employees continue to try to improve the organization. This small and almost invisible minority will be difficult to identify, unless you're a very careful observer. They are not loud and boisterous. They may seem to be plodders. But a few of them have been successful in making what they consider to be important changes. These employees have been rewarded by an occasional success, and they continue to try. However, a majority of employees have never tried, or they quit trying because they were unsuccessful. Some employees become so frustrated by the lack of change in the organization that they quit. Others stay on and adapt in their own way to working within boundaries, though at the cost of losing almost all initiative. Research in this area repeatedly confirms that organizational climate has a greater impact on employee satisfaction than actual job performance does.

Patterns of Adjustment

Consciously or unconsciously, people develop means of adjusting to the frustration caused by conflicting demands: they adjust in order to minimize their frustration. Human-service workers adjust in three general ways: (1) they identify with clients, (2) they identify with their jobs and coworkers, or (3) they identify with their organizations (Friedlander and Margulies, 1969; Lawler, Hall, and Oldham, 1974; Prichard and Karasick, 1973). These categories do not fit specific personality types; they describe various behavior patterns. As staff members change, their behavior changes. You will move from category to category during your career. By taking a closer look at these three general forms of adjustment, you will see that there is a range within each form. Maybe you can think of a coworker who fits one or more of the following descriptions.

Identifying with Clients

Reformers. These people see clients' needs as most important, and they try to work to change organizations in ways that will help their clients. They feel that professionalism and unionism are unimportant. These people tend to be vocal in staff meetings. They want to help the client first, and then fill out the forms. They want to stop the bleeding before they determine the patient's Blue Cross number. Most of the established staff members see them as radicals.

Innovators. Although they see clients as most important, they realize that their coworkers and their organizations need to be changed. They are active listeners, and when they speak, they ask questions. They aren't loud, and they are difficult to identify. The difficulty of spotting such staff members is documented by the fact that sex, age, and personal attitudes do not seem to predict innovative behavior in staff members in complex organizations. Baldridge and Burnham (1975), of Stanford University, tested earlier research indicating that young, cosmopolitan, educated people are likely to be innovators. They found that this was not the case in large public schools in both California and Illinois.

Victims. These workers feel that they are being frustrated by the system. They tend to fight the organization, and they may drag clients into the combat as allies. The extreme example of this employee type doesn't value either the organization or the standards of the profession. These staff members feel wronged and oppressed by the "evil" of the organization. They have decided to stay and fight, rather than run. They see themselves as heroes of the weak and helpless. In negotiations, these staff members represent the client; the supervisor represents the organization. Skilled supervisors deal with victims on a one-to-one basis in order to avoid attracting an audience of staff members, who might pick up some ideas regarding manipulating the system to benefit the client. This concept is detailed by Wasserman (1971), who also reports that, unless staff members who have chosen this means of adaptation can successfully mobilize the support of both their coworkers and their clients, they are forced to leave the organization.

Plodders. Though they identify with clients, plodders appear to have given up. They never complain. They seem to be good staff people, but no one really knows. They have accepted the conflicts and decided to live with them. They deal only with issues over which they have complete control. A teacher of this type may feel that "Once I shut my classroom door, I'm my own boss." A correctional officer who has adopted this form of adjustment might say, "When I am on the shift, they do it my way, even if it is different than the way the other guys do it." A security staff in an institution for delinquents says it this way: "When I'm in charge of the wing, I don't have to use lock-up to control the kids. I don't need it. It's just that I do things differently." A casual observer might assume that plodders would feel satisfied and involved if they had a chance to participate in policy making and administration. However, it has been shown that overparticipation in such activities can be dissatisfying (Conway, 1976). It depends on the individual staff member's need to participate and the organizational climate.

My Job: My Life. Many people are satisfied and fulfilled by their jobs as helpers. This is healthy, and it's the way it should be. Having a job that makes you feel productive and useful most of the time makes life better for you and your loved ones. However, it's unhealthy to use a job as a substitute for living. When your relationships with your clients overshadow your relationships with your partner or your child, you hurt both yourself and your clients. Your helping becomes confused with your own needs; the confusion leads to unwise choices. Clients become especially vulnerable to an increasing dependence on you that, because of your needs, you do little to discourage. It's not because you mean to hurt your clients; it's just that it feels so good to be respected and needed. Staff members are especially open to this behavior when a recent event has shown them that someone they cared for doesn't need them anymore. Most people need deep personal relationships; however, the use of clients to satisfy this need is not good for either the staff member or the client. The job histories of many professional helpers consist of a series of short-term direct client-service positions. Their search for a good job looks a great deal like a search for themselves.

Identifying with Coworkers

Staff members can adjust to frustration by identifying with other staff (the profession or the union). This identification takes two forms: amateur professionals and established professionals.

Amateur Professionals. These people are unsure of their skills and knowledge. They are unable to deal with their clients or their organization. They haven't integrated their own personal values with those of their profession. Their training and education have not given them self-assurance. They rigidly follow professional rules in order to avoid making mistakes. These employees talk about professional ethics, codes of conduct, and areas of jurisdiction. Rigidity in applying rules, regulations, and standards is their outstanding characteristic. They are often frantic—workers who have forgotten that the process of growing, learning, and healing is an ancient, complex, and natural process. A parallel can be drawn between amateur professionals and farmers: Farmers organize their work; however, once the crops are planted, they grow while the farmers sleep. No matter how hard the farmers work, they must wait for the seeds to germinate. The amateur professional has difficulty accepting the fact that natural processes take time, especially when all the best skills, tools, and techniques are used and all the right rules are followed. Blau (1960) refers to amateur professionals as local, as opposed to cosmopolitan.

Established Professionals. These people see themselves as members of a much larger and more important group than the organization that pays them. They belong to an organization of like workers. Blau calls them *cosmopolitan*. The union, the profession, or the national organization lies outside the agency. Although their primary loyalties are to these outside groups, they do not reject either the client or the organization. They resolve their conflicts with a superior attitude that seems to say, "If you people would only listen, my professional specialty has the answers to your questions."

Identifying with the Organization

Staff members can adjust to frustration by identifying with the bureaucratic organization. There seem to be as many descriptions of bureaucratic types as there are authors. One of the most interesting articles on this subject was written by Billingsley (1964), who details the differences between functional bureaucrats, job bureaucrats, specialist bureaucrats, and service bureaucrats. For our purposes, we will refer to all of these as *bureaucratic technicians*. Bureaucratic technicians treat the organization's policies and practices as supreme. No conflicts are real to them unless either the staff members or the clients threaten the rules and regulations. They carry out institutional procedures. In any conflict, institutional rules and regulations take precedence over professional standards and client needs. Kramer (1974) studied new nurses in hospital settings and concluded that a super-efficient bureaucratic-technician attitude is an extreme response to the conflict between school-bred values and work-world values. She speculates that the conflict between what new nurses have been taught and what they find is so great that, in order to survive psychologically, they reject the ideal values that are causing the conflict and adopt bureaucratic rules and regulations.

Conformists believe that the organization's policies and procedures are important; however, they also value professional standards. Conflicts between the two are either resolved as quickly as possible or ignored. Conflicts between staff members and the organization are very threatening to conformists; they try to resolve or hide such conflicts as quickly as possible. The conformist is the most common type of staff member; as a result, organizations have the continuity and stability they need to stay in business.

The value of getting along with other people and avoiding conflicts has been drilled into us from an early age. Our development and training have been reinforced by three major institutions: home, school, and church. Parents know what is right for their children. Teachers have the answers. The religious perspective is highlighted by peace and tranquility, if not outright acceptance without questioning. Robbins (1974) goes even further in supporting the notion that we basically fear conflict, hostility, and antagonism in his examination of the traditional philosophical teaching that conflict of any type is bad. Robbins talks about the United States as a peace loving nation. "Power for Peace" is the slogan of the U.S. Air Force. It is a tribute to human flexibility that any of us can view conflict as potentially positive or at least as neutral.

Who are you? Where do you fit—reformer, innovator, victim, plodder, amateur professional, established professional, or one of the bureaucrats? Maybe you are a combination of several types. Perhaps you don't fit anywhere in this list.

In this section, we have seen various forms of adjustment to the many frustrations that will confront you as a human-service worker. Your adjustment will, and must be, your own. The adjustments that you make on the job won't differ radically from the adjustments you make in other areas. If you are an unhappy person, you will probably be an unhappy worker. If you are frustrated at home, you will most likely be frustrated at work.

Staff Meetings

Most organizations provide formalized procedures by which administrators, supervisors, and staff groups can talk with one another. These usually take the form of staff meetings. Routine matters are generally handled in written communication through such things as announcements, memos, and posted notices. Usually, staff meetings are held on a regular basis. My experience has been that, when the person in charge of these meetings doesn't think that there is enough to occupy the group, information that would have been communicated in written form is reserved for discussion at the meetings.

Throughout your life, you have entered groups. The feelings you experience as you participate in your first staff meeting may resemble the feelings you experienced on your first day of school. There is usually a feeling of tension, because of the unknown. We have each learned to deal with this tension in our own way. Some of us have learned how to feel secure in new situations; we tend to focus on things that are familiar to us and comforting for us to see.

The importance of discovering the norms of the organization was discussed in Chapter 1. Staff meetings have their own set of norms and standards. These norms have been developed over a long period of time. If these norms are violated during the meeting, the group reacts to show that a violation has occurred. Usually, the violator is punished in some way, maybe by simply being ignored. A group without norms would have a difficult time in accomplishing its tasks. You need time to discover what your group's norms are.

Don't get carried away with the content of staff meetings. By content, I mean the items that are announced, the policies that are discussed, the cases that are analyzed, and the results of the decisions that are made. If you focus too much attention on the content of a meeting, you will lose your ability to see what is happening and how it's happening.

Process refers to what happens during a meeting and how it happens. Careful observation of the process will give you clues regarding the norms and standards of staff meetings. Who talks? For how long? How often? Whom do people look at when they talk? Who talks after whom? Who interrupts whom? Who responds to whom? What styles of communication are used (questions, claims, gestures, tones of voice, etc.)? Answers to these kinds of questions will help you to understand what's going on, such as who leads or who influences whom. How are decisions made? Are there votes, or does the person in charge of the meeting simply say, "Does anyone object?" or "We all agree, don't we?" Are decisions made by consensus? Is there a genuine attempt to encourage opposing points of view? Is conflict appropriate, or should it be handled outside the meeting on a one-to-one basis? Should you be honest with others and really tell them how you feel during staff meetings? Who are the people in the group that take on various roles? Who are the harmonizers—those who want to reduce tension and reconcile disagreements? Who are the encouraging members, who act friendly, warm, and responsive to others by either facial expression or remarks that indicate that they heard the other speakers? Who are the compromisers, who are interested in group cohesion? Who seems to set the standards and the norms? Who plays roles during staff meetings? You can answer these questions only by observing the process, rather than the content, of what goes on during staff meetings.

Most people find it difficult to listen to content and observe a process simultaneously. It will take practice on your part. You can practice by listening. It is very difficult to talk and observe at the same time. There are positive and negative consequences associated with being a quiet listener. One consequence is that it increases your ability to see what's going on. Another consequence is that your coworkers' first impression of you as a quiet person may cause them to treat you as if you have little to contribute. As a new employee, you probably are somewhat tense and aren't sure what your contributions are going to be or how they're going to be accepted. This insecurity on your part may be reinforced by the way in which other staff members treat you for being quiet. After you are more sure of the group's standards and norms, you will have a chance to correct this first impression. It is equally important that you re-examine your first impressions of your coworkers. Your impressions, as well as theirs, are probably incorrect. You have all become skillful at emotional role playing (Russo, 1965).

It isn't unusual for people to disguise certain feelings in order to conform to a socially acceptable model. When you met your coworkers, did you feel immediately that you would like some of them and prefer to avoid others? Did you find that some people instantly seemed warm and trustworthy, whereas others seemed cold and suspect?

First impressions are based largely on a resemblance to people who have been important in your life. Although such impressions may be quite inaccurate, they operate quickly and powerfully. We don't like a certain person—he senses our reaction to him and dislikes us. He turns out to be as disagreeable as we expected him to be. When we seek out the company of an individual we think we're going to like, the person responds to our interest and we find that we like each other. Our prophecy is confirmed. If we had treated the person we rejected as a promising friend, he or she might have become as congenial to us as the person we expected to like. We have mistakenly interpreted an accidental and incidental resemblance to someone else as our own intuitive talent—a talent that is likely to mislead us.

We are particularly misled when our pretended feelings cause us to lose contact with what we really feel. By observing, you may see people who seem quite anxious but claim that they feel comfortable. You might hear people ask questions on topics about which they don't really care. It is not surprising that people who have learned socially desirable behavior can pretend to others that they feel what they don't really feel. For some people, the years of practice at pretending have caused them to lose the ability to identify their real emotions.

Traditional Staff Categories

Nonprofessional, paraprofessional, and professional are standard labels. These labels do not necessarily reflect an individual's relative worth or competence. The term nonprofessional doesn't imply incompetence any more than the term professional implies excellence.

Nonprofessional

The nonprofessional staff includes those who are employed by your agency or organization who have a high school education or less. This is the group that is typically unionized and has a standard contract. Everybody in this group is hired, promoted, and paid according to established standards. The groundskeepers, janitors, maintenance personnel, bus drivers, cafeteria workers, nurse's aides, psychiatric ward staff, and delivery people are members of this group.

Paraprofessional

The paraprofessionals are those employees who, because of their specialized training, receive higher hourly pay than do the nonprofessionals. This group of staff people must account for their working time; that is, like the nonprofessional group, they are expected to work specific hours. If, for some reason, they are unable to maintain their schedule, there are standard reporting procedures dealing with work absence. Some of the employees in this group may be unionized or belong to some form of employee association. Included in this group are electronics-data-processing personnel, laboratory technicians (below the educational level of the registered medical technologist), purchasing agents, dispatchers, specialized machine operators, social-service aides, mental-health workers, child-care workers, and secretaries. The distinction between paraprofessional and professional employees is often blurred by the pressures placed on organizations to serve their clients; however, those who see themselves as professionals work very hard to maintain the distinction.

Professional

The professional staff category is composed largely of college-educated or professional-school-trained specialists. Their contracts are generally negotiated on an individual basis, though they may turn out to be very much alike. Professionals' work hours are somewhat more flexible than those of other employees. Until recently, professionals were not unionized, but they belonged to professional organizations, many of which are national in scope (such as the American Medical Association and the National Education Association).

Professionals are trained by specialized units in colleges and universities. These specialized units are usually called departments. Each of these departments has its own identity. Each chairperson in charge of a department has an office, a secretary, and a group of professors for whom he or she is responsible. In order to survive, each of these departments needs to maintain the identity of its discipline. Departments need budgets and students (clients), and they have to show production (student credit hours).

A friend of mine, sociologist Jim Henslin (1976), makes an excellent case that higher education, with its emphasis on production, is becoming more like a factory than an educational experience. Departments work very hard to maintain their identities, even though large amounts of overlap exist between such departments as psychology, counselor education, special education, community organization, social work, sociology, education, nursing, human development, rehabilitation counseling, behavioral science, urban studies, and human services.

The goal of each of these departments is to train people as human-service workers. As a result of the continuing struggle for survival, each department has developed and maintains a specialized professional jargon. Each has its own way of describing people, their problems, and how to help them. In order to keep their students, the department must believe that their specialty is critical to the identification and solution of human problems. This belief is communicated to students by faculty members. By the time the student is graduated, the new helper firmly believes that his or her own specialty is the most important of all of the helping professions.

Moreover, many college departments are staffed by nonpracticing specialists who are somewhat removed from the jobs they're training their students to perform.

Professors project their hopes, fears, fantasies, and ideals to their students. Most professors do this hoping that somehow their students will make changes in the way in which things are done and improve clients' services. However, many professors become confused regarding the difference between what ought to be and what is. Nonpracticing specialists teach "what ought to be" as though it really existed. Students graduate with an idealistic picture of the helping world, some technical skills, a lot of professional jargon, and the feeling that their specialty is most important. This overemphasis on specialization causes serious communication problems among professionals.

Communication Between Categories

Opportunities for communication between and across traditional staff categories will be less frequent, yet less formal, than the communication that takes place within your category. Until people from various categories get to know one another as individuals, stereotypes will be maintained.

An example of a communication problem is illustrated by this quote from a guard in a security institution for delinquents:

> For some reason or other, social workers and psychologists come in and give the impression to a youth supervisor that they are little gods that can solve anybody's problem, which really isn't true. They more or less gave a kid permission that whatever he did was all right for various reasons. They used all kinds of excuses for the kid: that he was brain damaged, came from a poor family, his mother was a drunkard, things like this that to me were nothing but crutches. I looked at it a little bit different than they did, I guess, because I figured that, out of all the kids that do live in ghettos, slum areas, the percentage of kids that get in trouble is far less than the kids that don't get in trouble. Quite a few kids out there are making it without being put in jail. It caused problems between the youth supervisors and the professional people. In fact, they threw up kind of a brick wall, and when you throw a brick wall up, you're not helping anybody.

The observation of a psychiatric aide working in a mental hospital demonstrates this negative attitude toward professionals—in this case, a psychiatrist:

I've never seen a doctor call a patient. I have always heard and had the impression that a psychiatrist is supposed to be a colleague and somebody relating to a patient, but I've never seen that happen. I mean, all that I've seen a psychiatrist do is walk up, open the nursing notes and the medicine charts, and write down "Thorazine, two hundred milligrams"—that's all he writes. And then he goes off and stays in his office. I don't know what the hell he does; he doesn't come and watch. He takes long breaks, whatever, but I've rarely ever seen him work with patients.

If you are among the professional group, I would encourage you to take time to develop relationships with nonprofessionals. For instance, the secretary is not paid to work with clients, but you will quickly discover that she or he influences both the administrators and the clients. In addition, secretaries have more information about what's going on in an organization than other staff members have.

In medical and psychiatric settings, the aides can often give the most accurate picture of the clients. They spend most of the working day in direct contact with clients and yet they tend to be overlooked as competent sources of information. The few professionals who make the effort to establish rapport can reap many benefits in providing quality client care. Communication between the people who work in the lunchroom, mess hall, or cafeteria and the other staff members is important. When clients are employed in the food preparation process, information flows from the cottage, classroom, ward, or cell block to the cafeteria through the clients. This information, like all information, can be helpful, harmful, or inconsequential to you, but you can assume that it won't be accurate and complete. A good relationship between the rest of the staff and the food-processing people can be invaluable in terms of special events, such as Christmas and Easter parties.

At times, client treatment programs can make use of specialized service-oriented personnel as part of a client-treatment team in very effective ways. A part-time job (and a good supervisor) is just what some clients need. You will see your own examples of ways in which nonprofessional staff members can be important in helping. Many nonprofessionals and professionals seek jobs in helping agencies because they genuinely like to help. Others consider their job as something to be tolerated—they wish to have as little contact with the clients as possible. The latter can be damaging to the very things that are most important to clients.

Communication between all levels of staff can make life pleasant and allow each staff member to provide the kind of care and help that should be available to clients. I recall a janitor in a small rural high school where I was a counselor. My office was very close to the boiler room, which was the janitor's "office." One day, shortly after a student had come to see me, the janitor came in and said, "I'm glad Henry came in to talk to you. I've been trying to get him to do that for months. He really has a lot of problems, and I was afraid he was about to kill his mother." By talking with the janitor, I discovered that he had been counseling with this student for almost three months; and, to my further surprise, I discovered that the janitor was carrying a "caseload" of about twenty students. He did not seek out these students. They came to him and he listened. He didn't give advice. He kept confidences. He was a nonthreatening observer of almost all of the student body's activities. It goes without saying that he was one of the greatest helpers I've known.

A public school teacher recalls the following advice from his student teaching days:

> Cultivate the right people for friends. Janitors, operators of the book store, and secretaries are often more useful than fellow teachers. This tip was impressed on me by my cooperating teacher. Her clean room, chats with the book store operators, and conversations with the secretaries were reciprocated by special favors from the janitors (they always opened her room for her in the morning), the book store (only she could get book orders for her classes on time), and secretaries (Mrs. Bennett knew everything worth knowing).

One public-school teacher describes her relationship with the janitor this way:

> The janitor in our building is fantastic. That man has done more for me and the people in our area than a lot of our administrators. Whenever there was a problem there, like he saw that maybe there was too much mud on the floor after he'd just waxed, he'd say, 'Will you kind of watch and . . .,' and I said, 'Sure, I'd be glad to.' We thought so much of him, we even bought him Christmas presents.
>
> The area that we're in was made for air conditioning, and it's just ungodly hot, very hot in warm weather. He fought to get us fans. In fact, I can remember, before we finally got them this year he went to the office and said, 'Hey, listen. Those teachers and students are dying up there. It is so hot that they can't survive.' And after school, at 3:00 or 3:20 when you'd get out, we'd sit around the lounge if we had things to do, and we'd wait till he'd come and he'd talk with us. 'Well, how was school?" and "How was class today?' You felt like he really gives a damn, you know. Maybe he's just being nice, but at least he is.

A public-health nurse talks about a secretary who has become very powerful over the years, to the point of controlling much of the activity of a public-health agency:

> She'd tell you you can't write any more on those appointment pages—the secretary was telling me this, you know, not the nurse, but the secretary. She almost ran the nursing department. She'd been there longer than anybody, so she knew all these little things that put her in a position to run the nursing department. So here were people who needed their baby's shots and different things. And when you'd be there, there'd be two or three nurses and a helper ready to work in this clinic, and a doctor and only a few people would show up. At the same time, she'd make people wait two and three months for an appointment.

Secretaries are key members of any organization. They often have information about what is going to happen before anybody else does. In many organizations, secretaries control schedules, payroll distribution, staff assignments, and information flow to administrators. The quality of your relationship with key staff members will have a lot to do with how successful you are on your job. A teacher describes a principal's secretary this way:

> She takes a lot of the fighting, arguing, and harassment that people direct at the principal. She's a very nice person. She knows what's going on. She knows where the papers are, what needs to be done. I mean, she runs the school to a certain extent, and she is a very nice person to have working for you. Any time that we get a memo and don't understand it, or we want to know something about the pay periods or doing homebound teaching, call Helen and she knows. She knows about travel expense, she knows about how to line buses up for field trips; all these things she takes care of and handles, and she answers all the questions. Decisions that, perhaps, the principal has made but hasn't got back to you yet; if it's on her desk, you know, you can find out.

Secretaries, janitors, aides, and maintenance staff are only four of the many kinds of personnel who work together. Especially in residential institutions, you will find a wide range of formal training and backgrounds among your colleagues. Staff members who have professional sounding titles, such as "counselor," "youth supervisor," or "cottage parent," may be English majors, retired heavy equipment operators, part-time bus drivers, or former company clerks. You have worked hard to get a formal education. It is likely that many of your fellow staff members will not have a degree. For those of you who believe you are specially trained, it may be difficult for you to understand how such people got their jobs.

Give these people a chance. You may find human beings with whom you can relate — people who have helping skills that you may lack.

In socioeconomic terms, most social workers, teachers, counselors, mental-health workers, police officers, and clergy have been socialized as middle-class people; many clients have not.

Socialization

There are many definitions of the term *socialization*. For our purposes, socialization refers to the process by which you learn all that you need to know in order to get along in the world in which you live. In the middle-class world, socialization includes learning to knock on the bathroom door when it's closed, minding your manners at the dinner table, and so on. If you learned these things as a matter of course while you were growing up, you probably take them for granted today. We develop many habits through socialization. "Habit is not original nature, but something added, as clothes are added to the body. Habit is added to nature by nature — the result of training and experience" (Russo, 1968:vii).

As a new employee, you are subjected to another stage of socialization. The organization that hired you wants to make you into as valuable a staff member as possible, and you want to use the organization for personal satisfaction. When the process works well, both you and the organization benefit. You are, or soon will be, subjected to "adult socialization" or *acculturation* by the organization (Schein, 1971:401). Nelson (1991) describes the three stages of a newcomer's adaptation to a new job as anticipatory socialization, encounter, and change.

Before we examine some studies of the institutional-training process, or socialization, it will be helpful to understand the relationship between norms, controls, and socialization. In the first chapter, norms were discussed. You will recall that norms are unwritten rules and guidelines that nobody really has to talk about; everybody understands them. Although norms are unwritten rules, some formal written rules may be related to norms. Take the simple example of the rule that requires you to report for work at 8 A.M. That rule is probably written down somewhere; however, the norm could differ from the rule. For instance, you may find that 8:20 A.M. is the latest acceptable time to arrive, and that 8:20 to 8:40 is coffee time, rather than work time. This is common in many one-shift organizations. Organizations that operate multiple shifts seven days a week — "total" institutions as Goffman (1961) calls them — may have a different norm for the 8 A.M. written rule. The 8 A.M. shift may be expected to be on the scene no later than 7:45 A.M. The fifteen-minute overlap may be used to effect a transfer of information from one shift to another.

In a small way, the extent to which you conform to norms regarding arrival time reflects the extent to which you have been socialized. What made you accept this norm? What controls affect you? Controls exert pressure on you to conform to the rules—to become socialized. At times, controls take the form of sanctions and punishments. In my experience, the controls on staff members who get to work too early do not fit a pattern, and, in some cases, being early doesn't violate any norms. Check it out, though; by arriving early, you might gain first-hand knowledge of some controls! Violation of the arrival-time norm on the late side always elicits controls of some sort, ranging from a bad look to a reduced paycheck.

This rather simple example demonstrates the relationship between controls and norms. Said another way, "The function of all control must be normative, i.e., to define, maintain, establish, or reestablish norms" (Millham, Bullock, and Cherrett, 1972:410). Millham and his associates provide a good description and explanation of various forms of control. Institutional control, control by orientation, informal control, and structural control are a few of their interesting categories. For those who work with clients in highly controlled situations, these authors offer ideas that may be of great material value. Each organization determines its own controls and the effects of those controls. Although it is risky at best to generalize to you and your organization, a few occupational specifics of this socialization stage—control—are discussed in the following paragraphs. Again, a word of caution—do your own research on your own organization.

Socialization of Social Workers

Social workers and social-work agencies have a wide variety of names and functions but they all have at least two things in common—paper forms and limited funds. The work socialization of social workers includes two seemingly contradictory attitudes regarding paper work. Forms and other paper work are discussed as though they are boring and useless—as though they interfere with the helping process to the point of dehumanizing the clients. On the other hand, office routines, such as filing and keeping records, are highly valued. One explanation for this apparent contradiction is that even the most committed workers sometimes find themselves emotionally drained by excessive contact and use the escape into bureaucratic paper work to preserve their own mental health (Wasserman, 1971).

Since organizations have limited funds, decisions regarding allocation are determined by detailed sets of rules. Most new human-service workers are surprised to find that they are advocates of their clients when dealing with their supervisors. You, the worker, are trying to get all the help you can for your client. Your supervisor is trying to protect the agency's budget. To help your clients, you may need to learn to "work the system" in some questionable ways. You may overlook a client's part-time job, or report that a child has a behavior disorder so that his or her family can collect a few additional dollars of much-needed support.

The press to accept these kinds of attitudes can lead to an uneasy feeling of guilt associated with "unethical" behavior or frustration if you follow the rules. "The social worker in such a bureaucracy is caught up in this brutal intersection of contradictory values" (Wasserman, 1971:95).

This description of the socialization of social workers confirms the early research of such people as Francis and Stone (1956) and Green (1966). In a detailed case study of a social work organization, Francis and Stone found that, contrary to classical theory, "The evidence in one area after another did not sustain the notion that bureaucracy implies impersonality and rule-following" (Francis and Stone, 1956:13). Francis and Stone reported that, although rules were seen as impediments in the way of service to clients, if the workers felt that the clients did not deserve more, the procedures and office rules were used to support the workers' judgment. This was especially true of social workers who felt that hard work and an honest day's labor is more worthwhile than homemaking. While a student in the School of Social Science Administration at the University of Chicago, Green (1966) wrote a paper describing the conflicts created within social workers by the organizations that pay them. Although he didn't use the term socialization, Green detailed a variety of pressures and choices faced by the new social worker, including the careful evaluation of anticipated rewards and their sources—the profession, the clients, the agency, or the community. Unless you watch carefully, such choices may be made for you by other staff members as they do their part to socialize you.

The Socialization of Teachers

Since the days of the one-room schoolhouse, teachers have been subjected to an intense socialization process. Along with the home and the church, the school remains one of society's major means of transmitting its culture to its youth. In our era, in which many traditional values are being questioned, teachers are caught in a series of value cross-fires. For example, the Sierra Club supports values that place the environment before profit. One of their goals is to encourage teachers to adopt this value. On the other hand, teachers are subjected to the traditional view that a capitalistic system depends on profit. This latter view maintains that the goal of public schools should be to increase the productive capacity of young people by helping them to develop social skills, technical competencies, and motivations that are appropriate in a capitalist society. Bowles and Gintis (1976), of the University of Massachusetts, claim that the purpose of public schools is to legislate inequality and perpetuate the expropriation of the products of labor as profit for stockholders. These kinds of value decisions will confront the new teacher as a part of the socialization process.

Of all the helping professions, teaching has been studied most intensively in terms of the socialization process. The literature on the socialization of classroom teachers can be placed in four categories: early childhood experiences, the influence of important models, peer influence, and students as socializing agents.

The psychodynamic process begins early in the future teacher's life. Ben Wright, the leading exponent of this position, even discounts the student-teaching experience as simply a continuation of the early fantasy-like ideas regarding teaching (Wright and Tusha, 1968). In a series of articles, Lortie (1966, 1968, 1969) argues that some pupils become teachers as a result of childhood experiences. Lortie claims that the potent models of teachers are internalized by their students. One of the characteristics of effective models is that they possess power. Teachers certainly possess power over children. Smith and Geoffrey (1968:49-50) describe a teacher's own personal belief system and its influence on classroom behavior. As one reads Smith, it is apparent that he is discussing the influence of early experiences with teachers that the novice teacher displays in his or her own classroom behavior. Smith emphasizes the socialized belief, at least at the elementary level and in high school athletics, that pupils "belong" to a teacher and have a responsibility to that teacher for their behavior, even when they are not with that teacher. This belief has been passed on from generation to generation and has apparently become a part of the school culture.

A comprehensive review of research on the problems of beginning teachers was done by Veenman (1987). The focus of that review was to design programs and measures to reduce the reality shock for the new teachers. The emphasis was to alter the teacher training curriculum to prolong the tenure of high quality classroom teachers with the overall aim of improving education. Veenman's work was preceded by Wubbels et al., (1982) when they identified the roots of the experiences creating reality shock in beginning teachers. The focus of the Wubbels research was to modify pre-service training, especially for physics teachers. Marso and Pigge (1986) found that secondary teachers experience more reality shock than do elementary teachers, and teachers employed by urban schools have much more reality shock than those employed by rural or suburban schools.

In a study done in Australia, McArthur (1979) concluded that teacher adjustment from early career optimism to the reality of the classroom situation was not as traumatic as previously reported. This conclusion is supported by Power (1981) with a longitudinal study in the United States looking at selected student-teacher characteristics and the extent of change in those characteristics during transition to beginning teacher. Again, contrary to expectations the data showed considerable stability calling into question the theories of new teacher reality shock.

The socialization effect of other teachers and supervisors is powerful, because they are what Edgar and Warren (1969) call "sanctioning colleagues." A sociological study conducted by Lortie (1975:72), *School Teacher*, detailed the socialization pressure on new teachers with special emphasis on the first year of teaching. In partial agreement with Edgar and Warren, Lortie reports that new teachers turn to other teachers for informal exchanges of opinions and experiences.

Haller (1967) supported the view that the most powerful socializing agents for teachers are students. The influence of children on the process of making a person a teacher is evident to me each time the local kindergarten teacher talks to me as though I were five years old. She has adopted the language and much of the other social behavior of her kindergarten students.

The Socialization of Nurses

Nurses, like teachers, are semiprofessional in the sense that they are employed on rather standard contracts. Nurses and teachers are also similar in that they "tend to have horizontal occupational structures located in vertical multilevel organization hierarchies" (Alutto and Belasco, 1974:226). In other words, chances for advancement in an organization are slim for teachers and nurses. This absence of professional advancement opportunities encourages many teachers and nurses to leave their professions (Alutto and Belasco, 1974; Kramer, 1974). Over 70 percent of male teachers intend to leave the classroom (Lortie, 1975:87), and women see their continued teaching as contingent on events in their lives outside their occupation (Lortie, 1975:99). In both teaching and nursing, the career system favors recruitment into the profession, rather than retention. This practice results in low personal involvement and commitment on the parts of large numbers of professional people in these fields. Like all socializing agents, these low-commitment types will encourage new employees to accept and adopt their views, attitudes, and norms. Remember, low-commitment employees see an informal shadow organization that differs from the shadow organization seen by dedicated and committed employees.

Those of you who plan to be nurses will see a contrast between low-commitment R.N.'s and high-commitment L.P.N's and aides. Kramer (1974) describes the socialization role that aides play with regard to new R.N.'s. Many new nurses were surprised to find that these aides have so much experience and knowledge about the organization. (New nurses may find Kramer's classic book well worth reading.) Since Kramer's classic work, more studies have been done, and nurse training processes have been revised. Recent efforts at providing mentors and other forms of job-coaching have reduced their level of reality shock for the new nurse. Bradby (1990a) studied in some detail the process of the transition from student into the occupational role of nurse. She found the transition was easier for those with higher self-esteem and lower anxiety. In a similar study, Bradby (1990b) describes in more detail the aspects of patient care most relevant to reality shock for the new nurse.

The Socialization of Police Officers

Most police recruits, or "green peas," are highly motivated and committed to the department (Van Maanen, 1975). They want to be effective members of the team and enforce the law according to their academy training. This high commitment of police recruits is in vivid contrast to new "fish," or new prison guards, who view their careers as a long series of temporary jobs (Jacobs, 1974). Police recruits are subjected to "the speedy and powerful character of the police socialization process resulting in a final perspective which stresses a 'lay low, don't make waves' approach to urban policing" (Van Maanen, 1975:207). In fact, officers who clung to high expectations were found by Van Maanen to be least likely to be evaluated as good police officers by their sergeants, whereas those with the least favorable attitudes were rated as better performers.

The initial high team spirit of police recruits is refined by the socialization process once they become members of squads. The members of each squad are assigned a specific geographic area; they are expected to back one another up, cover for one another, and share the work load. New officers who are "too committed" can create additional work for other squad members.

Several variables influence the outcome of the police socialization process. The recruit's attitudes towards crime and punishment are one variable (Fielding and Fielding, 1991). Moral values (Domalewski, 1988) and authoritarianism have all been found to be related to socialization outcomes. For example, Brown and Willis (1985) found that in a group of recruits in the United Kingdom, on-the-beat experience led to a dramatic increase in authoritarianism when that beat was in an area with a high crime rate. On the other hand, low crime rate areas with an emphasis on community policing did not produce the same impact on the new officer.

Socialization in Human-Service Occupations

Six general points can be made regarding socialization in human-service occupations. These points relate to educational preparation, the sequence of socialization events, the identification of new employees, the probation period, trainers, and the "no rat" rule.

Educational preparation. Your educational preparation (academy, college, orientation sessions, or training programs) may or may not be useful in your new job as a human-service worker. Some of what you've learned in school won't fit. This is the real world you're in now.

The sequence of socialization events. The sequence of socialization events begins with the recruitment process and ends with either termination or successful socialization. These events serve to maintain the status quo in an organization.

The identification of new employees. New uniforms, special classes, and crowded offices are a few of the physical characteristics that tell the established employee you're new on the job.

The probation period. The longer the probation period, the more demanding and degrading it can be. During this test period, your socialization will be evaluated by your trainers, coaches, and managers. They will determine your success on the basis of your acceptance of the norms, standards, and attitudes that keep the organization running as it has always run. You know whether you've failed in your socialization efforts — the result of failure in this area is isolation.

Trainers. Professors, teachers, instructors, and preceptors are all trainers. On your new job you will have a coach. It is sometimes difficult to identify coaches, because they may not be formally assigned to their roles. Your officemate, the teacher across the hall, the aide who works your shift, or a client may act as your coach.

The "no rat" rule. The "no rat" rule is common to all organizations. It is considered risky for any employee to "tell on," "gig," or "squeal on" another employee. It is especially risky for a new employee to rat on an established employee.

Volunteer Staff Members

As a human-service worker, you will be working with volunteers. Volunteers can be either a big help or a pain in the neck. A volunteer program that includes good recruitment, selection, training, and supervision can be a big help to you. Maybe the volunteers can do a portion of your job that you'd rather not do. When volunteers are present, you might do those things that you always wanted to do but never had time. The one thing all volunteers have in common is time to give. When you work with volunteers in a partnership, you might find that you have more total human contact with clients. Moreover, you may find volunteers who have skills and experiences you lack.

The Growth of the Volunteer Movement

Hundreds of thousands of agencies in the United States have volunteer programs. Perhaps you work for one of these agencies or are a volunteer in an agency. Volunteerism is not new; however, in recent years, the idea has caught on.

An increased demand for services, shorter work weeks, longer life span, and higher levels of unemployment and homelessness have all added to the volunteer movement. Approximately ninety million adults are involved in some form of volunteer service to other people giving three hours a week on average (Driver, 1989). Agency budgets are being restricted as the competition for tax dollars becomes more intense. Requests for the expansion of paid staff positions fall on deaf ears. Meanwhile, some people have more time on their hands than they ever had before. The majority of these people are middle or upper class. They are the ones who volunteer — people who need to be needed by and involved with others. Most of us have a desire to count, to make a difference in somebody's life. As paid jobs become more scarce — especially for college graduates — more and more young people are finding that one of the best means of obtaining a job in an agency or institution is to do volunteer work. It gives them practical experience (something to add to a future job application) and an opportunity to be on the spot in case an opening occurs in the agency in which they are volunteering their time.

Pros and Cons

My experience in nine organizations has been that the majority of volunteers have significant contact with many community resources through their families, churches, clubs, and friends. Often, such contacts can be used to help you and your clients. It can become a bit sticky when you find yourself supervising a volunteer who is of higher status in the community than you think you are.

Aside from the direct advantages to you and your clients that are made possible by volunteers, the community education and organizational visibility that volunteers provide can help to support requests for new facilities, a larger budget, and program expansions.

The specific roles that volunteers have in your organization will depend on the type of clients you serve and the skills and competencies of the volunteers. Volunteers in the field of juvenile probation are being used in roles that range from administrative clerks to diagnostic psychologists (Scheier, 1971). Volunteer recruitment, screening, and training materials are available from the National Volunteer Center of the Points of Light Foundation, 736 Jackson Place, Washington, D.C. 20503, (202) 408-5162.

Let's look at the other side of this issue. Volunteer programs have been troubled by high turnover rates, lack of commitment from paid staff, low volunteer dependability rates, poor record keeping, and bad management in general (Scheier, 1972:33).

Most of the weaknesses of volunteer programs concern the following issues:

1. Paid staff believe that volunteer programs reduce their control over clients.
2. The "friend to the client" role of the volunteer can cause conflict with the paid staff.

3. Rather than serve more clients better, paid staff want to have more control over the programs they now have.

4. High turnover rates among volunteers cause problems for clients.

5. Poor orientation and supervision of volunteers is common.

6. Recruitment and selection practices are inadequate.

7. There are too many volunteers, and there is not enough to do.

8. There are too few volunteers.

Even if your organization has a poorly run volunteer program, you may have an opportunity to use the volunteers assigned to you. But wait—don't try to reorganize the entire volunteer program. Do that later. In order to use your volunteers effectively, you will need to:

1. Be specific and clear about what kinds of help you need to better serve your clients.

2. Select those needs that the organization allows volunteers to fill.

3. Determine in which of these needs your volunteers are most interested.

4. Establish a *regularly* scheduled time to meet person-to-person with the volunteers.

5. Be honest—tell it like it is when you talk with your volunteers.

6. Listen—the volunteers may have some ideas that haven't occurred to you.

7. Both you and the volunteers need to make and keep careful records of activities—especially client contact.

Paid staff in your organization may have negative attitudes regarding volunteers. These staff members may have developed these attitudes as a result of experience. Don't argue with them or try to make them change their attitudes. The best way to help them change is to demonstrate the effective use of volunteer staff. Even that may have no effect if the presence of volunteers in the organization threatens them. Some staff members may be made uncomfortable by volunteers who are intelligent and of high social class. On the positive side, suppose that everything the volunteer does and says is good! But be careful—are you breaking any organizational norms with your good volunteer program? If so, you need to decide whether breaking the norm to obtain the volunteer service is worth the price that you may have to pay.

Due to the nature of their positions, volunteers can afford to take more risks than paid staff members can. They have a source of livelihood independent of the organization. This is especially true of national volunteers, such as members of VISTA, who don't work in their home communities. Risk taking can be very productive. One VISTA volunteer was responsible for starting one of the first youth emergency services in my local area. It has now grown to encompass a wide geographic region. A part of this service is supervised and professionally supported by the local mental-health professionals, who take turns carrying an electronic call beeper when the mental-health clinics are not open. Volunteers call the professionals when they need their help or counsel with a client.

Conclusion

"Are volunteers really effective?" is the wrong question. More appropriate questions might be: "Under what conditions are volunteers effective?" Or, "Who is the target of help—the volunteer or the client?" After reading the suggestions for the effective use of volunteers in the preceding section, you have a general idea of what makes an effective volunteer program. The helper therapy principle is well documented. Slow readers in the fifth and sixth grade, when given the opportunity to tutor first and second graders in reading, increase the reading level of not only the first and second grade clients, but their own reading level. Institutionalized delinquent youth who voluntarily act as therapeutic visitors to institutionalized geriatric mental patients show a significant improvement in self concept scores (Russo, 1971). Incidentally, the geriatric mental patients also showed improvement, but not at the level of statistical significance. More recently, Guinan et al., (1991) reported that emotional support volunteers working as caregivers for people with AIDS were rewarded with feelings of personal effectiveness, emotional support, social support, and empathy/self-knowing. Clary and Orenstein (1991), when studying the difference between volunteers who completed their nine-month service commitment to those who quit early or were screened out, found that those who continued exhibited more altruistic motivation than those who did not complete their commitment. A two-year study of a volunteer tutoring program (Morris, Shaw, and Perney, 1990) demonstrated that the use of volunteers in helping at-risk, primary grade children learn to read made a statistically significant differ-ence. The use of volunteers as counselors for high-risk, young male offenders showed better success than a matched group of offenders on regular probation. The differences were especially dramatic when one compared the low-risk group to the high-risk offenders (Moore,

1987). Before one would begin a volunteer program, the abilities of the volunteers, the job description, and the client needs and perceptions should be examined and matched as closely as possible. For example, in a study by Morrow-Howell et al., (1990) that examined the effect of racial composition of the volunteer-client dyad, it was found that the racial composition of the dyad had a significant effect on the helping relationship. Specifically, black volunteers serving black clients committed more time and were seen as more helpful by clients than black volunteers serving white clients.

Summary

Each of us has built a set of selves for various social situations. Our parents coached us on how to behave when particular relatives came to visit. We learned patterns of behavior that have been more or less effective in dealing with teachers and parents. The lifelong process of socialization teaches us various rules of conduct, values, and attitudes, as well as behaviors that we use to fulfill our social obligations. These become so much a part of us that we are not fully conscious of the choices we make. When we enter the social situation of a new job, we present the social self that we "choose." This choice becomes a factor in the adult socialization process that is about to begin. The organization is attempting to transform us into valuable employees, and we want to use the organization for our personal satisfaction. Coworkers play a key role in this socialization process. Staff meetings provide one opportunity for the socialization of new employees.

Discussion Questions

1. What changes would you like to see on your job or in your school? Are they important enough to do something about? How much would it cost to make the changes? How much is it costing you not to try to make the changes?

2. How would you describe the organizational climate where you work or go to school? To what extent does this climate affect you and your performance?

3. Where do you fit in the adjustment patterns discussed in this chapter? Are there patterns that weren't discussed? How have you adjusted to your present position in school or at work? How much of the "victim" is in you?

4. What forces and models operated in your socialization? To what extent does your behavior conform to that of the significant people in your life?

References

Alutto, J. A., and Belasco, J. A. 1974. Determinants of attitudinal militancy among nurses and teachers. *Industrial and Labor Relations Review*, June, 27(2).

Baldridge, J. V., and Burnham, R. A. 1975. Organizational innovation: Individual, organizational, and environmental impacts. *Administrative Science Quarterly*, June, 20.

Billingsley, A. 1964. Bureaucratic and professional orientation patterns in social casework. *Social Service Review*, December, 3(4), 400-407.

Blau, P. M., Wolf, V. H., and Stauffer, R. E. 1960. The structure of small bureaucracies. *American Sociological Review*, April, 31, 179-92.

Bowles, S., and Gintis, H. 1976. *Schooling in Capitalist America*. New York: Basic Books.

Bradby, M. 1990a. Status passage into nursing: another view of the process of socialization into nursing. *Journal of Advanced Nursing*, October, 15(10).

_____. 1990b. Status passage into nursing: Undertaking nursing care. *Journal of Advanced Nursing*, December, 15(12).

Brown, L., and Willis, A. 1985. Authoritarianism in British police recruits: Importation, socialization or myth? *Journal of Occupational Psychology*, June, 58(2), 97-108.

Clary, E. G., and Orenstein, L. 1991. The amount and effectiveness of help: The relationship of motives and abilities to helping behavior. *Personality and Social Bulletin*, February, 17(1), 58-64.

Conway, J. A. 1976. Test of linearity between teacher participation in decision making and their perceptions of their schools as organizations. *Administrative Science Quarterly*, March, 21.

Domalewski, R. M. 1988. Selected Moral Values. Dissertation — Abstracts International, The Humanities and Social Sciences, February, 48, 8.

Driver, D. E. 1989. *The Good Heart Book*. Chicago, IL: The Noble Press, Inc.

Edgar, D. E., and Warren, R. L. 1969. Power and autonomy in teacher socialization. *Sociology of Education*, 42, 417-26.

Fielding, N. G., and Fielding, J. 1991. Police attitudes to crime and punishment: Certainties and dilemmas. *British Journal of Criminology*, 31(1), 39-53.

Fletcher, J. 1966. *Situation Ethics*. Philadelphia: Westminster Press.

Francis, R. G., and Stone, R. C. 1956. *Service and Procedure in Bureaucracy: A Case Study*. Minneapolis: University of Minnesota Press.

Friedlander, F., and Margulies, N. 1969. Multiple impacts of organizational climate and individual value systems upon job satisfaction. *Personnel Psychology*, 22, 171-83.

Goffman, E. 1961. *Asylums*. New York: Doubleday.

_____. 1969. *The Presentation of Self in Everyday Life*. Garden City, NY: Doubleday/Anchor.

Green, A. D. 1966. The professional social worker in the bureaucracy. *Social Science Review*, 40(1), 71-83.

Guinan, J. J., McCallum, L. W., Painter, L., Dykes, J., et al. 1991. Stressors and rewards of being an AIDS emotional-support volunteer: A scale for use by care-givers for people with AIDS. *AIDS-Care*, Vol. 3(2) 137-50.

Haller, E. J. 1967. Pupil influence in teacher socialization: A socio-linguistic study. *Sociology of Education*, 40, 316-33.

Henslin, J. M. 1976. University as a factory. In J. M. Henslin and L. T. Reynolds (eds.), *Social Problems in American Society*. Boston: Holbrook Press.

Hoffer, E. 1967. *The Ordeal of Change*. New York: Harper & Row.

Jacobs, J. B. 1974. *The making of a correctional officer: 1974*. Unpublished mimeograph, Illinois Department of Corrections, February.

Kramer, M. 1974. *Reality Shock: Why Nurses Leave Nursing*. St. Louis: C. V. Mosby Co.

Lawler, E. E., III, Hall, D. T., and Oldham, G. R. 1974. Organizational climate: Relationship to organizational structure, process, and performance. *Organizational Behavior and Human Performance*, 11, 139-55.

Lortie, D. C. 1966. Teacher socialization: The Robinson Crusoe model. In *The Real World of the Beginning Teacher*. Report of the Nineteenth National TEPS Conference, Washington, D.C.: NEA, 54-66.

_____. 1968. Shared ordeal and induction to work. In Howard S. Becher (ed.), *Institutions and the Person*. Chicago: Aldine.

_____. 1969. The balance of control and autonomy in elementary school teaching. In A. Etzioni (ed.), *The Semi-professions and their Organization*. New York: Free Press, 153.

_____. 1975. *Schoolteacher: A Sociological Study*. Chicago: University of Chicago Press.

Marso, R. N., and Pigge, F. L. 1986. *Beginning Teachers: Experience vs. Realities*. Annual Conference of the Association for Supervision and Curriculum Development. San Francisco, CA. March.

McArthur, J. 1979. Teacher socialization: The first five years. *Alberta Journal of Educational Research*, December, 25(4), 264-74.

Menges, R. J. 1975. Assessing readiness for professional practice. *Review of Educational Research*, Spring, 45(2), 173-207.

Millham, S., Bullock, R., and Cherrett, P. 1972. Social control in organizations. *British Journal of Sociology*, December, 23(4), 406-21.

Moore, R. H. 1987. Effectiveness of citizen volunteers functioning as counselors for high-risk young male offenders. *Psychological Reports*, December, Vol. 61(3), 823-30.

Morris, D., Shaw, B., and Perney, J. 1990. Helping low readers in grades 2 and 3: An after-school volunteer tutoring program. *Elementary School Journal*, November, Vol. 91(2), 133-50.

Morrow-Howell, N., Lott, L., and Ozawa, M. 1990. The impact of race on volunteer helping relationships among the elderly. *Social Work*, September, Vol. 35(5), 395-402.

Nelson, D. L. 1990. Adjusting to a new organization: Easing the transition from outsider to insider. *Prevention in Human Services*, 8 (1), 61-86.

Power, P. G. 1981. Aspects of the transition from education student to beginning teacher. *Australian Journal of Education*, November, 25(3), 288-96.

Prichard, R. D., and Karasick, B. 1973. The effects of organizational climate on managerial job performance and job satisfaction. *Organizational Behavior and Human Performance*, 9, 126-46.

Robbins, S. P. 1974. *Managing Organizational Conflict: A New Traditional Approach*. Englewood Cliffs, NJ: Prentice-Hall.

Russo, J. R. 1965. Emotional role playing. *Group Process: A Teaming Method*. Delinquency Study Youth Development Project, Southern Illinois University, Edwardsville, IL.

_____. (ed.). 1968. *Amphetamine Abuse*. Springfield, IL: Charles C Thomas.

_____. 1971. *Final Report: Delinquents as Therapeutic Visitors to Mental Patients*. Grant 5-9-236098-0059, U. S. Office of Education (HEW).

Scheier, I. H. 1971. *Volunteers in Court: A Manual*. USDHEW-SRS (72-26007). Washington, DC: U.S. Government Printing Office.

_____. 1972. *Guidelines and Standards for the Use of Volunteers in Correctional Programs*. U.S. Department of Justice (LEAA), Stock 2500-00236. Washington, DC: U.S. Government Printing Office.

Schein, I. H. 1971. The individual, the organization, and the career: A conceptual scheme. *Journal of Applied Behavioral Science*, 7, 401-62.

Smith, L. M., and Geoffrey, W. 1968. *The Complexities of an Urban Classroom: An Analysis Toward a General Theory of Teaching*. New York: Holt, Rinehart & Winston.

Van Maanen, J. 1975. Police socialization: A longitudinal examination of job attitudes in an urban police department. *Administrative Science Quarterly*, 20.

Veenman, S. 1987. *On Becoming a Teacher: An Analysis of Initial Training*. Conference on Education of the World Basque Congress. Bilbao, Spain. October 13-17.

Wasserman, H. 1971. The professional social worker in a bureaucracy. *Social Work*, January, 16(1), 89-95.

Wubbels, T. and others. 1982. Research notes: Training teachers to cope with the 'reality shock'. *Studies in Science Education*, Vol. 9, 147-60.

Wright, B. D., and Tusha, S. A. 1968. From dream to life in the psychology of becoming a teacher. *School Review*, 76, 253-93.

5 Community Based Programs

The role of the human-service worker is continually evolving as governmental and societal changes occur. Mental illness, mental retardation, crime, poverty, ignorance, and physical disabilities have always existed. The human-service and educational institutions and organizations that provide services have emerged through a historic process which seems to have cyclic tendencies.

Historical Context

In colonial America, crime and poverty were not seen as indications of defects in community organizations but rather were accepted as a natural phenomena. Communities were self-policing. Criminals were placed in stocks, publicly whipped, or branded in such a way as to signify the offense. In addition to inflicting pain, the intent was to establish and enforce social controls. As long as people lived in closely knit communities with very few transients, such systems operated quite well.

Acceptance of the poverty-stricken was encouraged by the clergy as an opportunity for well-to-do individuals to exercise Christian virtues by giving to the poor. The poor included widows, orphans, the mentally ill, the mentally retarded, and physically disabled people. When the numbers of these "worthy" poor became too large to be housed in private residences, the institution of the *almshouse* emerged. Churches and volunteer organizations were responsible for these institutions as well as for the majority of other health, education, and welfare functions.

As the population grew, so did the crime and poverty rates. Jails were built to house common criminals and the criminally insane. School houses were built and teachers hired. Local community support gave way to state support. Mental hospitals "grew in size, absorbing the denizens of the jails and poorhouses" (Appelbaum, 1987:5). These hospitals began as a humanitarian attempt to treat people with mental illness more effectively than was considered possible in the community. Unfortunately, overcrowding and underfunding quickly became the reality and such institutions often became mere holding units in which only custodial care was given.

The Great Depression provided the motivation and the basis for the majority of our current government operated help-giving organizations. The massive failure of the economic system plunged millions of otherwise self-supporting people into poverty. The crushing demand for social services was beyond the resources of private charitable organizations, and existing state and local governmental agencies proved inadequate. Partly as a result of this inadequacy, the Social Security Act of 1935 was passed. This act clearly indicated the direct involvement of the federal government in the welfare of its citizens. The first large-scale federal involvement in mental health, the National Mental Health Act (NMHA) was passed in 1946. This act provided an intellectual and financial source of innovation in mental health training, research, and practice.

There certainly was a great need for immediate federal assistance, but unfortunately, bureaucracy tends to take a significant amount of time to get fully underway. Throughout the 1950s, state asylums remained overcrowded and understaffed. The conditions were often deplorable. Gradually the institutional environment became more therapeutic and humane as state and federal authorities gained more awareness and control. Attempts to manage the overpopulation of the mentally ill patients began in the 1950s with small numbers of patients transferring to other types of facilities or being discharged. Thus began the "deinstitutionalization" movement which became much stronger in the 1960s.

Deinstitutionalization

The word "deinstitutionalization" has been given many definitions, most of which have been vague or incomplete. One of the better definitions is "the shunning or avoidance of traditional institutional settings, particularly state mental hospitals, for chronic mentally ill individuals, and the concurrent development of community-based alternatives for the care of this population" (Bachrach, 1989).

The move toward deinstitutionalization occurred in other institutional environments as well as in mental health (which will be discussed in the following section). In the mid-1950s, for example, the state of Massachusetts attempted to close all of its residential juvenile corrections facilities and to shift the placements of youths to community-based and smaller custodial care facilities. About this same time, the California Youth Authority became active in community-based treatment for youthful offenders. Today, the federal government regularly advertises for private contractors to house adult federal prisoners. In addition, there are several sets of circumstances in which the federal government becomes responsible for juveniles. During the late 1980s and early 1990s, for instance, there was a population of minors who entered the country from Southeast Asia without either parent. They became the responsibility of the federal government. Through private contractors, sometimes called service providers, there are thousands of such persons being cared for at several levels of security. There are private maximum security institutions as well as minimum-security halfway houses.

The deinstitutionalization trend has also impacted general hospital populations. The advent of outpatient surgery and the dramatic reductions in the length of hospital stays have contributed markedly to patients being moved from the large hospital environment to home or community-based care.

During the "no new taxes" atmosphere of the late 1980s and early 1990s, federal and state budgets were increasingly strained and cuts were often made at the expense of human services. Thus, much of the responsibility for the mentally ill, mentally retarded, and other needy people has been returned to the family and community, similar to the ways of colonial times (Appelbaum, 1987; Rochefort, 1989).

The Mentally Ill

The most dramatic example of deinstitutionalization has occurred in the area of mental health. This process actually began in 1955 with the Mental Health Study Act of 1955. This act financed a comprehensive study of existing services for the mentally ill. The final report led to one of the last pieces of legislation signed into law by President John F. Kennedy in 1963. President Kennedy gave the following message (in part) to Congress:

> I propose a national mental health program to assist in the inauguration of a wholly new emphasis and approach to care for the mentally ill. This approach relies primarily upon the new knowledge and the new drugs acquired and developed in recent years which make it possible for most of the mentally ill to be successfully and quickly treated in their communities and returned to a useful place in society.
>
> These breakthroughs have rendered obsolete the traditional methods of treatment which imposed upon the mentally ill a social quarantine, a prolonged or permanent confinement in huge, unhappy mental hospitals where they are out of sight and forgotten. . . . and at the same time upgrade mental health services. (Mandell and Schram, 1985).

Shortly after this message to Congress, the Community Mental Health Centers Act of 1963 (CMHC Act) was enacted. It called for outpatient clinics to be developed in every area of the country with the local facilities responsible to federal authorities. These centers were to be a major catalyst in the facilitation of liberating patients from the constraints of institutional life. Though deinstitutionalization did occur to a large extent, the local Mental Health Centers did not play the expected role. Many such centers were never built and those that were provided treatment for the more desirable, easier to treat population rather than the chronic, severely mentally ill (Appelbaum, 1987; Rochefort, 1989).

Today, the residential population in state mental hospitals is one-fifth of what it was in 1955. While this sounds impressive, many of these patients were re-institutionalized into other types of settings, some of which may be less satisfactory than the original placement. A large number of the elderly chronically mentally ill are in nursing homes. Many of the younger population have been placed in community residential care settings. Some have slipped through the cracks and make up a disproportionate percentage of the homeless population (Bachrach, 1989; Oskamp, 1989; Shadish, Lurigio and Lewis, 1989; and Rochefort, 1989). A small number who had the financial ability turned to private psychiatric and general hospitals.

Unfortunately, it is not the patient's diagnosis that determines where he or she is treated or for how long, but rather the patient's economic status and personal goals (Lewis, et al., 1990). This socioeconomic class inequality evident in the differential treatment of mentally ill is the root of many current policy dilemmas in human services.*

State Mental Hospitals Today

State mental hospitals continue to serve as a back-up for those clients who can not be placed in the community or who have returned after a failed attempt to survive outside the institution. "These cases include chronic deteriorated patients, actively aggressive and assaultive patients, and some individuals suffering from a combination of mental and physical illness so severe as to tax local facilities" (Rochefort, 1989:329). The treatment may be primarily custodial for some of these patients, or it may be on an acute basis for those who fail to obtain community aftercare services and who often become "revolving door admissions." Some patients require the structured setting that is available in a hospital environment but often not present in community facilities.

Unfortunately, state institutions are often deteriorated, antiquated buildings in isolated areas of the community. The quantity and quality of staff tends to be insufficient, due to high turnover, limited pay, and inadequate funding.

The original objectives of deinstitutionalization were to close the state hospitals and to provide adequate community care. Neither has been met. One-fifth of the 1955 residential population remains in these facilities. This number seems to have stabilized, so the closing of hospitals is not realistic in the foreseeable future. "There has been failure to provide alternative care in non-institutional settings, failure to reintegrate chronic mental patients into the community, failure to dramatically improve their quality of life, failure to reduce their dependency on mental health and social welfare institutions, and often failure to provide simple custodial functions for needy patients" (Shadish, Lurigio, and Lewis, 1989:6).

Torrey (1988) puts it this way:

1. There are at least twice as many seriously mentally ill individuals living on streets and in shelters as there are in public mental hospitals.

2. There are increasing numbers of seriously mentally ill individuals in the nation's jails and prisons.

---

*A further source of information is the "Handbook on Mental Health Policy in the United States," referenced at the end of this chapter.

3. Seriously mentally ill individuals are regularly released from hospitals with little or no provision for aftercare or follow-up treatment.

4. Violent acts perpetrated by untreated mentally ill individuals are increasing in number.

5. Housing and living conditions for mentally ill individuals in the community are grossly inadequate.

6. Community mental health centers, originally funded to provide community care for the mentally ill so these individuals would no longer have to go to state mental hospitals, are almost complete failures.

7. Laws designed to protect the rights of the seriously mentally ill primarily protect their right to remain mentally ill.

8. The majority of mentally ill individuals discharged from hospitals have been officially lost. Nobody knows where they are.''

A policy which may have begun as a noble endeavor has turned into quite a disaster. The situation can only be turned around through hard work, planning, research, community and family support, and concerned advocates.

Nursing Homes

The number of institutionalized elderly mentally ill decreased 79 percent between 1965 and 1979. Most of the patients were transferred to nursing homes, making nursing homes the largest single setting for the mentally ill. Several factors facilitated this move from larger state institutions to nursing homes. Psychotropic medications controlled much of the bizarre and violent behavior. Court decisions gave patients more rights, making it easier for them to choose to leave the institutions. Some patients had physical conditions requiring more intensive care than was available in facilities less restrictive than nursing homes. For some, the only economically feasible option was a nursing home. Thus many elderly mentally ill patients were transferred into nursing homes with little real planning.

Nursing homes have always been geared toward physical illnesses. Unfortunately this means that the staff members are rarely trained to deal with mental illness. Because of this, problems are often overlooked, misdiagnosed, or patients are overmedicated to produce submission. Custodial care tends to be the primary objective, much like the institutions which the deinstitutionalization movement had hoped to eliminate.

Medicaid began to provide financial support for mental patients transferred from state hospitals to nursing homes in 1965. The states were able to receive 50 percent or more from the federal government for their cost of care. Thus, nursing homes became a less expensive alternative to institutions. Medicaid regulations in the 1980s stipulated that no more than 50 percent of the patients in a nursing home can have psychiatric diagnoses, excluding organic mental conditions. Many patients go undiagnosed because of this regulation. There have been estimates that as many as 75 percent of the patients are actually mentally ill. Without an official diagnosis, the condition goes untreated.

The move toward deinstitutionalization occurred before adequate outpatient supportive services were developed. As a result, as many as 10 to 30 percent of the elderly people in nursing homes could probably function as well or better in the community if proper support services were available. Hopefully this community support will become available so those people can be placed in the least restrictive setting.

Community Residential Care

Nursing homes provide care for the largest number of mentally ill people. The next two major care-giving systems are state institutions and the community residential care settings which are estimated to house an approximately equal number of residents. The community residential care facilities are divided into three primary types.

Family Care Homes. Six or fewer mental patients living in the community with a private family is called "Family" or "Foster" care. In this setting a social worker or other professional provides supervision for the caretaker who supervises the residents. This type of community care was one of the first attempts as an alternative to the institution. The number of residents in this type of program has remained relatively small. The Veteran's Administration has used it more than any other group with about eleven thousand mentally ill patients in foster family care.

Board and Care. The original purpose of this type of setting was to provide a bed, board and care. A lack of uniformly enforced national standards has led to a wide disparity in the quality and type of care provided. Some of the facilities are treatment-oriented.

Others provide a warm family-like environment. Then there are some that are as substandard as the stereotype suggests. The negative images of exploitation, abuse, and neglect certainly do exist, but not to the extent that the press would have people believe. The negative stereotype has resulted in decreased funding, and therefore fewer beds, even though there is a great need for board and care facilities which are the least expensive supervised housing option.

Satellite Housing. This setting provides more independence than either family care homes or board and care. Small groups of two to five mentally ill residents live together in an apartment, duplex, or small single family home. Residents are responsible for the general housekeeping chores and for paying the rent. Supervision is available for guidance and counseling as needed. There may be several housing units in a specified area or an entire building may be leased out for this purpose. Several units of the building may get together for group meetings, with or without the supervisory staff. Social integration and independence are encouraged in this housing arrangement, yet it is used very little in this country.

A lack of affordable housing for the mentally ill is a major problem. Providing this housing is important for economic reasons, as community residential care is much less expensive than institutionalization. Even more important is the quality of life for the deinstitutionalized patients, which these care settings have the potential to greatly improve. Unfortunately this potential has not yet been met due to inadequate funds, lack of proper monitoring, community hostility to area facilities, insufficient number of beds, and the negative stereotypes that the media has stimulated (Rochefort, 1989).

Homelessness

"Deinstitutionalization, sometimes referred to as 'dumping,' has been cited as the reason for the increasingly large numbers of homeless women and men seen on our city streets. Theoretically, there was to be a discharge plan for every individual. Unfortunately for those without families or other support this usually consisted of carfare to the nearest welfare office" (Rousseau, 1981:19). The deinstitutionalization process certainly contributed to the homeless population but is not the sole factor. An estimated 30 to 40 percent of the homeless are severely mentally ill (Fustaro, 1984; Morganthau, et al., 1986; Rochefort, 1989; Rousseau, 1981).

"Many of these former patients drift about unprotected and

unprovided for on the streets. Although sent to welfare or the Social Security offices, they often become 'lost' only to turn up in emergency rooms or to be seen sleeping in public places" (Rousseau, 1981:19). The stigma against the mentally ill and, to a lesser extent to the mentally retarded, limits job and housing opportunities. Some of the homeless lack the skills or permanent address to get into the Social Security or welfare systems.

Ten federally-funded research studies shared the following descriptive information:

1. The homeless mentally ill are most commonly a multi-need population, with substance abuse, physical and mental health problems, and vocational and social deficits.

2. There tend to be histories of residential instability, and currently they have few housing options open to them; however, they do not move frequently between localities.

3. A surprisingly large group of homeless mentally ill is involved with the criminal justice system, both as victims and as perpetrators.

4. Homeless mentally ill persons are usually willing to accept assistance. However, service providers' perceptions of clients' needs often differ from the clients' perceptions. Clinicians tend to focus on the need for specialized mental health interventions, whereas homeless mentally ill tend to emphasize the lack of basic housing and social supports. These differences in priorities may be wrongly interpreted by service providers as resistance to receiving help (Rochefort, 1989). Homelessness has always been a problem but as the number increases, so does visibility. People are becoming more aware of it as the media dramatizes their plight every winter, triggering further investigations of causes and possible solutions, none of which seem very effective (Fustaro, 1984).

Our society tends to be indifferent, to look the other way until an incident occurs which forces our attention. The incident can be as tragic as the mentally ill lady who was set aflame by four teenage boys in 1978 (Rousseau, 1981) or as benign as seeing someone sleeping in the bus station. In either case, the homeless, and especially the mentally ill homeless, spark feelings of embarrassment, annoyance, sympathy, anger, helplessness, and many other emotions depending on one's attitudes and experiences. Most people recognize that something needs to be done, but no one seems willing to take the responsibility.

Common legal standards require that a person be a proven danger to himself or others before he or she can be involuntarily admitted to a mental hospital. "The rights of patients are important, but their illness must be considered as well. Liberty to be psychotic is not 'freedom' in any responsible sense of the word" (Morganthau et al., 1986). Even voluntary admissions are difficult to achieve. Deinstitutionalization has pushed many people onto the street with few or no options open to them. E. Fuller Torrey, M.D. states that what is needed is a combination of the following:

1. The seriously mentally ill must get first priority for public psychiatric services.
2. Psychiatric professionals must be expected to treat individuals with serious mental illness (as compared to mildly ill patients who are easier to treat and more financially rewarding in many cases).
3. Government responsibility for the seriously mentally ill must be fixed at the state or local level.
4. Housing for the seriously mentally ill must be improved in quantity and quality.
5. Laws regarding the mentally ill must be amended to insure that those who need treatment can be treated.
6. Research on the causes, treatment, and rehabilitation of serious mental illness must increase substantially (Torrey, 1988).

If these recommendations were carried out, one third of the homeless would disappear. They would be in supervised living facilities, taking medication regularly, and some would be working. There would be a perceptible decrease in prison populations. Many of the individuals would require only temporary hospitalization for medication regulation and stabilization. "Finally, the quality of life for individuals with serious mental illness and their families would improve substantially" (Torrey, 1988).

Outreach Programs

The Community Support Program, established in 1977, was the major federal response to the care of people with severe mental illness. Added to Torrey's six recommendations was an outreach program. Professionals who work in outreach programs must have a set of skills that can be practiced in the client's home environment. Such environments are seldom controlled by middle-class norms. Outreach workers are faced with decisions that affect their personal health and safety. At minimum, outreach workers must be able to perform the following activities:

1. Engage clients in a helping relationship (a process that can take up to several years of aggressive and persistent contacts and offers of assistance).

2. Assess client's health, mental health, substance abuse, housing and welfare needs.

3. Intervene in crisis situations (e.g., acute psychiatric episodes, health emergencies, or social welfare or personal crises).

4. Refer clients to appropriate health, mental health, substance abuse treatment, housing, and social welfare agencies. Many outreach programs also provide ongoing assistance to clients in meeting basic needs such as food, blankets, medication administration, or first aid (Rochefort, 1989).

The seventeen billion dollars in public funds spent on mental health services in 1985 probably would be sufficient to provide excellent care of the seriously mentally ill if the money were used wisely. Studies have shown that good services for such individuals living in community facilities cost no more than mediocre services in state hospitals. "Rehabilitative services for the seriously mentally ill can also be cost effective by decreasing the need for hospitalization and, for those able to work, decreasing utilization of support programs such as SSI" (Torrey, 1988).

Like the mentally ill, mentally retarded individuals have been deinstitutionalized into private group homes and other settings which range from excellent to mere custodial care (Landesmann-Dwyer, 1981; Hemming, Lavendar, and Pill, 1981).

Increasing numbers of outreach programs are being developed to deal directly with other major social problems, such as AIDS. For example, HIV positive newborn babies must be kept in hospitals for room and board unless community programs are available. Specialized foster parent programs are operating to care for HIV positive infants, many of whom also have needs stemming from maternal drug abuse during pregnancy.

Roles for Human-Service Workers

A wide variety of human-service professionals work in community-based environments. Among the challenges facing these professionals is maintaining good relationships with other members of the community. Community programs and the people who run them deal constantly with the N.I.M.B.Y. ("not in my backyard") phenomenon — local residents often support a program in concept, but they are resistant to efforts to locate a group home or halfway house in their neighborhood.

There is, and will continue to be, a great need for qualified, dedicated people to work with the deinstitutionalized population. The work can be demanding, requiring patience, creativity, and good judgment. Much of this population has potential, yet their abilities have often been stymied by a poorly conceived and executed deinstitutionalization process.

It is important for human-service workers to realize that the quality of their clients' lives depends upon a variety of factors other than their specific illness. The material needs for food and shelter that were once met by an institution may now be met in a group home. Your role, even though you may not have the title of case manager, will involve helping your client access housing (if needed), social security disability benefits, food stamps, Aid to Families with Dependent Children (AFDC), General Assistance (GA), and so on. For those clients with financial resources, many options of care are available. The human-service providers also work for those who can afford to shop and pay for the services they desire.

There are a variety of positions in community-based agencies that may be of interest to you. They include (but are not limited to): adult reading teachers, psychiatric aides, mental health technicians, activity and recreational therapists, psychiatric nurses, occupational therapists (registered, assistants, and aides), social workers, case workers, psychologists, and psychiatrists. Most of these require specialized training. The role of outreach workers has been briefly described. This is probably one of the most difficult and most frustrating positions. It is also probably the most needed, and may be the most rewarding. Opportunities for employment in such programs cover a wide array of professions. The increasing use of community resources such as specialized foster care will require the training of volunteers. Training and continued support for these "community providers" requires a multi-disciplinary staff, some of whom may even act to provide respite services for such direct care givers. Nursing homes, halfway houses, board and care homes, and others mentioned are admittedly far from perfect. Professional staff are required in all of these facilities. You can be a factor in improving the quality of life for this group of people. By overcoming the public's indifference, change can be made, benefitting not only the mentally ill, but all of society. You, as a human-service worker, can be involved in such changes. Temper your enthusiasm and idealism with a carefully developed set of information that can be used in a systematic strategy for change.

Volunteer Boards and Paid Staff

Increasing numbers of beginning human-service workers will accept positions with private providers. These are nongovernmental agencies typically controlled by volunteer boards of directors. There is a proliferating use of local groups to run programs aimed at achieving the policy goals of government planners. Traditionally, these community organizations have drawn their vitality, influence, and participatory character as informal social organizations. These boards have often been by-products of church activities or as expressions of neighborhood unity. Some of them began in ethnic enclaves of large cities or in isolated rural towns. Many of these local, self-help organizations have become engaged in achieving specific policy objectives in collaboration with some agency outside the community that can provide them with financial resources. As the reliance on outside resources increases, the organizations become larger, they employ more professionals like yourself, and become more concerned with pleasing these external agents who make the funding decisions. These private agencies tend to become more bureaucratic — operating procedures are written down and formalized. A few professionals become responsible for making most of the decisions and for directing other people.

Members of the local community may find it more difficult to keep abreast of all of the details in the organization's activities as this professionalism increases. Community volunteers are likely to become less involved in the decision-making processes as professionals like yourself working on a day-to-day basis take greater responsibility for planning. This dynamic tension between you, your fellow staff members, and your volunteer board may often be uncomfortable, but it also provides an opportunity for continued growth and development. Participatory community organizations are difficult to keep going but appear to provide one of the most effective vehicles available for delivering services relevant to community needs.

These voluntary community organizations are usually strongly committed to active democratic participation. Consequently, deciding what to do is often slow and cumbersome. As a new professional staff member, you are likely to feel frustration with the apparent slowness of this decision-making process. This democratic participation may make it hard to move quickly to pursue opportunities for outside grants and contracts. Such opportunities are successful often in terms of how quickly and efficiently your organization can produce certain services or products. Again, the challenge of the professional is to live with and use this creative tension to better serve your clients.

Organizational Continuity

Your organization, if it is run by a volunteer board of directors, will likely face conditions of instability. Crises usually stimulate periods of rapid growth with publicity, volunteer interest, and more financial resources. If crises are not properly managed, a board will often lose members because they have been overused. But such crises often produce a new pool of potential board members to invest their time, energy, and perhaps money. Part of the stability must be provided by a professional leadership structure that is held responsible for the organization's performance. Again, there will be tension between the professionals in the bureaucracy and the volunteers from the community. The goal is to blend the stability and confidence generated by the professionals in such a way as to promote full participation by volunteers.

By focusing attention on the achievement of specific goals, rather than the process of participation, a bureaucratic organization can promote a concern for efficiency and rationality. Yet voluntary organizations are irrational in the sense that everyone has a personal reason for explaining what they are doing and why they are doing it. This may result in inefficiency that, though frustrating, is the heart of why voluntary organizations are valuable (Milofsky, 1982).

Summary

In colonial times in the United States, the poor, the mentally ill, and the criminal were taken care of at the community level. With the Great Depression and its accompanying economic disasters, the federal and state governments accepted much of the responsibility for the care and custody of this part of the population. Beginning in the 1950s, the trend was reversed and the movement toward deinstitutionalization began. This movement occurred in mental health and corrections and, to a lesser extent, in education. The move toward community involvement and the responsibilities that are associated with it continue to show promise of providing more efficient and effective support and services for improving the quality of life for that part of our population. Little progress has been made, however, in producing an organization of services that are truly effective. Those of you who work at the entry level position in education, mental health, social services, and the physical health arena will be constantly frustrated by your inability to link your students and clients with the multiple services they require in addition to those that you can provide. Attempts at such service integration have been less than successful. Concepts like networking, interagency committees, and case management have become part of our professional jargon.

Increasingly, educational and other human services are being delivered by private contractors. These range from very small agencies operating limited programs in a small geographic area to statewide and even national for-profit organizations. The latter may be awarded contracts for the provision of services heretofore under the direct control of either the state or federal governments. Many of you, therefore, will be employed by such private agencies. These agencies are typically governed by a board of directors. Some of these boards are strongly committed to active democratic participation. Others are simply the rubber stamp for an executive director. This range of management styles will have differential effects on your job.

Discussion Questions

1. In the community where you live, work, or attend school, are there homeless people and, if so, where do they "live"?
2. Where were these people before they became homeless?
3. What percentage of your state's human services budget for direct care is being contracted to private agencies?
4. Are private organizations more efficient and effective in delivering education and human services?

References

Appelbaum, P. S. 1987. Crazy in the streets: The policy of deinstitutionalization. *Current*, October.

Bachrach, L. L. 1989. Deinstitutionalization: A semantic analysis. *Journal of Social Issues*, 45 (3), 161-71.

Fustaro, S. 1984. Home on the street. *Psychology Today*, February, 18 (2), 56-63.

Hemming, H., Lavendar, T., and Pill, R. 1981. Quality of life of mentally retarded adults transferred from large institutions to new small units. *American Journal of Mental Deficiency* 86 (2), 157-69.

Landesmann-Dwyer, S. 1981. Living in the community. *American Journal of Mental Deficiency* 86 (3), 223-34.

Lewis, D., Riger, S., Rosenberg, H., Wagenaar, H., Lurigio, A., and Reed, S. 1991. *Worlds of the Mentally Ill: How Deinstitutionalization Works in the City*. Southern Illinois University Press: Carbondale, IL.

Mandell, B. R., and Schram, B. 1985. *Human Services: Introduction and Interventions*. New York: John Wiley & Sons.

Milofsky, C. 1982. Professionalism in community organizations. *Community Action* 1 (3), 38-42.

Morganthau, T., Agrest, S., Greenberg, N. F., Doherty, S., and Raine, G. 1986. Abandoned. *Newsweek*, January 6, 14-19.

Oskamp, S. 1989. The Editor's Page. *Journal of Social Issues*, 45 (3).

Rochefort, D. A. 1989. *Handbook on Mental Health Policy in the United States*. New York: Greenwood Press.

Rousseau, A. M. 1981. *Shopping Bag Ladies*. New York: Pilgrim Press.

Shadish, W. R., Lurigio, A.J., and Lewis, D. A. 1989. After deinstitutionalization: The present and future of mental health long-term care policy. *Journal of Social Issues*, 45 (3) 1-15.

Torrey, E. F. 1988. *Nowhere To Go: The Tragic Odyssey of the Homeless Mentally Ill*. New York: Harper & Row, Publishers.

6 The Other Establishments

If you are employed by a human-service agency, your experience has shown you that some agency policies and practices don't help either you or your clients. You have seen administrators mess up. Perhaps you can identify the staff members with whom you enjoy working—and those you avoid, if possible. Your inflated expectations of the job have settled into a daily reality. As you strive to deliver services, you may begin to wonder whether all organizations are as poorly operated as yours. They can't be, you say—if they were, the system wouldn't work at all.

Since few agencies can provide all the services clients need, you will work with other human-service organizations. Your experience with other agencies may lead you to reevaluate your opinion of your organization. You may begin to feel a little better about your agency once you see how other organizations operate and witness firsthand the difficulty of coordinating services between agencies. The experience of one worker illustrates this point:

> This one lady, after I had gotten her name, address, social security number, and all of that kind of stuff, started to scream at me when I asked her how many kids she had and what their ages were. My first reaction was one of surprise, but when I got further into it with her, I realized that this was the fifth time this month she had been asked all of this same information. This mother was really looking for help and had run into this constant

barrage of the same questions probably asked in different order, in different ways. If I hadn't had taken the time to listen to her, she might have been written off as "uncooperative." Somehow we have to get these computer programs of the courts, family services, the unemployment office, and welfare to talk to each other.

It has long been recognized that the sheer size and complexity of the human-service system discourages clients from seeking help, and in many instances contributes to a worsening of client problems (National Commission on Children, 1991).

Size and complexity has been identified as a significant barrier to service integration. The multiplicity of agencies, programs, etc. make any efforts at inter-program linkages extremely complex (Yessian and Kvaal, 1991). It is virtually impossible to conceptualize the variety of ways in which coordination might occur and the even greater variety of difficulties faced by coordination attempts. The difficulties created by the size and complexity of the system are further exacerbated by bureaucratic inertia in involved agencies, a tradition which encourages red tape, delay, and complex and conflicting rules and regulations unique to each agency (Kidwell and Gottlober, 1991).

Referral

You have a client who needs a service that your agency can't provide. Your rules and regulations tell you how to seek referral help. The referral regulations most likely tell you to go to (or send people to) your supervisor. Your supervisor goes to the boss, who then goes to the big boss of your agency, who communicates to the big boss of the other agency, who goes to a supervisor to get a key staff person to contact either you or your client. Often, you aren't told that your client has been contacted; moreover, the referral process has taken so long that you've probably forgotten about the original contact. Even if all of the proper people are notified with a minimum of delay, the help that your client needs may come too late.

"Human-service systems" has become a popular phrase. Usually, when people think of the word "system," they think of coordination, a unitary whole, and comprehensive assemblage. The problems of coordination, integration, and cooperation among service institutions and agencies have not been solved. Twenty years of services integration efforts were reviewed by the Office of Inspector General, Department of Health and Human Services (Yessian and Kvaal, 1991). Like the weather, everybody talks about them, but nobody seems to be able to change them. Each organization has its own goals, procedures, and clients. Each has its own turf. Everybody believes that everybody else ought to change. Even radical social workers are slow to change their methods. Despite the fact that poor coordination exists, you have, or will have, clients who need the services of agencies other than your own. You can't rely on "the system" to secure help from other agencies for your clients.

Efficient and experienced human-service workers have built their own network of agency contacts. These personal networks are a logical consequence of the conflict that is built into the system. Many agencies compete with one another for a share of limited government funds. Some agencies compete with one another for office space. Most important, each agency has its own goal — its reason for existing. At times, various agency goals appear to be in conflict with one another, or, at a minimum, act to interfere with one another's service to clients. Examples include school policies that automatically fail students who are absent a specified number of days. Such policies will need to be modified if the goal is finding ways to keep young people in school. Another example is eligibility guidelines that exclude pregnant women from participation in certain drug treatment programs.

Different Agencies; Different Priorities

Individuals who work for a state mental-health agency may be formally concerned about the mental health of all the people in the state; however, they are told that their first priority is to reduce the long-term populations in the state mental hospitals. As a result, the state mental-health agency's first priority is the community placement of every patient it can possibly remove from the hospital. The social worker who works with the welfare department has clients who are not yet hospitalized and need counseling help. These clients may face long waiting lists, transportation problems, child-care issues, and a concern for their personal appearance at the new agency.

Therapeutic help for public-welfare clients is simply not a high priority for the state mental-health department. That department is being judged by its ability to reduce hospital populations. The priorities that are directed downward from the budget makers to the board, and from the board to the director, affect the way in which each help-giving organization looks at clients. Very real budget problems would result if the priorities imposed by those who control the agencies' money were ignored.

In addition to budget pressures, each agency has its own set of goals for its clients. Most religious organizations are interested in clients from birth through death, with special emphasis on the soul. Much like a vocational-rehabilitation agency, a church's interest extends beyond immediate service to its clients. Both the church and the rehabilitation agency have goals that are *longitudinal*, or future-oriented. Compare this orientation with that of a medical hospital and a probation department. The medical hospital's goal is accomplished when the patient is cured; the probation department's goal is accomplished when the client's sentence is completed. These agencies' interest in clients is less future-oriented than that of the church.

A second way to view an agency's service goals for clients is to consider how much of the client's life is of concern to the agency. Organizations that operate residential facilities — *total institutions*, as Goffman (1961) calls them — deal with the entire life space of each client, from moral beliefs to physical cleanliness. In contrast, due to the way in which most secondary schools are organized today, teachers may see as many as 250 students each day. They focus on the academic concerns of their students. This narrow focus is a consequence of the crush of numbers; most communities expect a much broader focus. Many responsibilities that traditionally were assumed by the family — such as sex education, personal counseling, and career development — are now considered to be functions of the school. School boards have responded by hiring specialists, each of whom sees hundreds of students. Despite the illusion of concern that is produced, the main focus is still academic. When a student doesn't make it in the academic system, agencies that have a broad focus take over. Foster homes, detention homes, and reform schools deal with the entire life space of a client. Public schools and total institutions have differing *lateral* views of clients — one is narrow, and the other is broad (Lefton and Rosengren, 1966).

It may help you to look at these organizations in terms of how they view clients longitudinally and laterally. Much interagency conflict results from differences in these views. The worker from the mental-health clinic who asks the teacher to "understand" a student may be met with, "Understand him? Hell, I wish someone would understand me." Many teachers who deal with as few as thirty students per day consider "social work," "psychology," and "mental health" to be dirty words — far outside their range of responsibility (Smith and Geoffrey, 1968:213). Many workers who deal with student dropouts see teachers' narrow academic concerns as the cause of the dropout problem.

Each organization views its clients in a particular way; this could help to explain the lack of interagency cooperation. Although the social caseworker who provided the following input did not see the problem from this angle, she realized that her client was not being served:

> There was an intake on a child. The parents had called Mental Health and told them that they wanted this particular child of theirs institutionalized. Mental Health passed the buck on to us. It was not our problem. If we had passed the buck back to Mental Health, we would have been in trouble anyway. We couldn't win for losing. So we dealt with the case as best we could and got it to the point where we gave this woman enough resources to effectively deal with Mental Health so that she could get some action from them. It took several hours of our time. That's one way I learned that Mental Health wasn't functioning, and on a primitive level. Then, in another case I had, the caseworker had actually referred the woman to Mental Health. The woman wouldn't go to Mental Health, because she was afraid to leave her house. She was that sick. So we got the kids out of the house. We did that. But Mental Health is supposed to have resources, as I understand it, for visiting caseworkers or visiting therapists. There was no such resource available. Mental Health was also supposed to have resources for transportation. It didn't. So I would go and sit and talk with this woman and try to help her.

Her clients were not being served by the mental-health agency in any meaningful way. On the other hand, the mental-health agency may have been achieving its own goals.

Rehabilitation agencies receive "points" for returning formerly disabled people to work. The number of clients that a rehabilitation agency can return to self-sufficiency is a statistic that a board understands. Difficult and long-term cases require more time than other cases. With severely limited staffs and facilities, rehabilitation workers are careful in choosing their clients. Other private and public agencies and institutions may not think that rehabilitation is doing its job, especially when those other agencies are unable to refer poor-risk clients to be helped. Each agency tries to limit the kinds of clients it accepts.

Frequently, social workers deal with clients who need legal aid. Social workers and lawyers are in the business of helping clients, but there are real differences in their areas of concern and their methods. Lawyers are concerned with their clients' legal rights—a relatively narrow perspective, both longitudinally and laterally. Social workers deal with the welfare of their clients in relation to society. Lawyers act as clients' representatives in court; social workers establish a professional relationship with their clients in an effort to change the clients and their environment. Often, conflict results when a lawyer and a social worker try to work together to help a client. A social worker related this experience:

> One of the problems we had was a woman who absolutely, religiously believed that divorce was wrong and that she would be bedeviled if she divorced. She was told by Legal Aid that she could have help to get a divorce, but not a legal separation. She needed the legal separation to keep her husband from coming into the house and beating up her kids and her.

At this point, you might feel that referring your clients is a lost cause. The time needed to go through the required steps in each agency is bad enough; when another agency is finally contacted, they may reject your request. If another agency accepts your request, you might not approve of their form of help. A family caseworker puts it this way:

> Legal Aid is swamped with cases, just like our agency is swamped with cases, and so is Mental Health. And so everybody's all swamped with cases, and everybody's pushing everything off on everyone else that they can. And what it really comes down to is the individual who's working with that family. What can that one individual caseworker do? Is that caseworker willing to invest the time and the energy and the hassling with Legal Aid or threatening them by saying, "This is an extreme case, and otherwise we'll have to remove the children from the home."?

There is another way to make referrals and get help for clients. Remember the nurse in the correctional institution whose clients needed medical treatment in hospitals? She discovered how to get around much of the bureaucratic red tape—she called cases "emergencies." A more common referral process involves the use of personal networks or "who you know." One experienced helper says:

> If you know a specific person with whom you're kind of friends, and you say, "Look, I really don't know what else to do, and I know that you can help with this situation. Is there any way you could free yourself up to do such and such?" If you have a friend, do something like this. I've got friends like that at Public Aid. I'll say, "Hey, their caseworker is doing nothing. Who do I go to? What do I do?" And they'll tell me who to go to, and they will tell me the structure, when it's involved. But also they might even do it themselves. It's not like these things are just available. It's a lot of hard work, and it's partly hit and miss.

The development of a personal network of referral resources requires time. Established employees may be reluctant to share their network with you. This reluctance is due, in part, to the fact that these networks are built on reciprocity. I help you and your client; you help me and my client. Employees who share their networks with you may be creating an obligation to be fulfilled later.

Interorganizational Cooperation

Every human-service worker has a special horror story that illustrates the lack of cooperation and communication among service agencies. A little town where I once lived planned to build a Youth Center as a delinquency-prevention measure. Included in this structure would have been bath facilities, a gymnasium, and a game room. The town had two fully equipped structures that were not usually occupied during the times when the proposed Youth Center would have been busiest. These structures were public schools.

Since schools are found almost everywhere, and most of us have spent at least a decade or two in them, they are convenient and familiar examples of less-than-ideal helping institutions. Nonetheless, public schools hold the most potential for early problem identification and the subsequent delivery of solutions. Chamberlin (1984) discusses the need for teachers to be aware of signs of inner conflict, and "must know how and when to use outside resources in the study-diagnosis-treatment process." Many of the problems students have require the help of specialists.

You may find yourself cast in the role of case manager. One of your challenges will be to integrate the services available so that your clients can access them. You will find this a real challenge.

> I was given this referral from the junior high school. On the surface of it, it looked pretty simple. Tim had been absent a lot, and when he did come, he wore the same raggy clothes, and was suspected of having a learning disability. Tim lived with his mother who worked the afternoon shift at the nursing home. He had an older brother who was eighteen now and was a drop-out. Tim says he does a lot of drinking. Tim had been expelled from school because of his truancy but had intercepted the mail at home so his mother didn't know about it. Tim's older sister, Alice, was pregnant Tim thought but didn't want to tell her mother. Tim's mother was taking a course at the local community college to brush up on her reading and writing so she could pass a test for a promotion at the nursing home. Through Tim, I got to talk

to his sister, Alice. Sure enough, she was pregnant and was afraid to tell her mother and wouldn't go with me to the clinic at the welfare department. She finally told her mother who took a day off from work without pay. When Alice got to the clinic, she wanted to ask some questions, but everybody seemed so much in a hurry and all they wanted to do was get answers to put on their form. Alice went down to the welfare office then and sat and waited a long time, and they asked her the same questions. Anyhow, when Alice's son was born, he weighed less than three pounds. It turned out that Alice was six months pregnant before she got any help. Anyhow, to make a long story short, the baby was real cranky and tough to take care of. The subsidized infant care at the church just couldn't handle the low birth weight baby. Although I had gotten Alice a slot in the GED training program, she had been absent so much to care for the baby that she lost it. Boy, it's been tough to try to coordinate the services, the welfare department, the clinic, the job training center, the volunteer tutoring services, and the school, but this is what a case manager is supposed to do.

Interagency partnerships have the potential capacity to harness the large and permanent funding channels that support our major educational, judicial, and other human service institutions. Even after these linkages and partnerships have been created, substantial new funding will be necessary to bring integrated services to sufficiently large numbers of clients to make a real difference.

The people who lead, participate in, and eventually implement integrated services are central to a successful program. Their vision, commitment, and competency as leaders will influence the process of negotiating a practical shared vision. These leaders will press each side to understand the other's point of view and the way they perceive the issues at hand. Such leaders will generate alternative solutions and pursue those that constitute common ground. It is often possible to balance the views and interests of one's own organization while working to guide the group, but leaders who attempt to do so must be especially sensitive to the perceived conflict of interest that can occur. Frequently, those who are able to avoid such conflicts have a broad-gauge, general background or cross-disciplinary training and experience that helps them to interpret and communicate issues from various points of view and pose solutions in such a way that multiple interests are served.

Creating linkages among multiple legal, educational, and other human service organizations requires not just one leader, but many — each working in concert with the others. As the process of establishing a shared practical vision evolves, members must simultaneously anticipate the kinds of resources, expertise, and political influence necessary to meet their objectives. High-level sponsorship with its attached visibility can also attract broad-based participation.

Key staff must translate the shared vision into quality service delivery, but innovations will make demands on your professional training and existing skills and abilities (State Reorganization Commission, 1989).

Service integration obviously requires cooperation among agencies, although there is often resistance to the change which occurs as part of service integration (State Reorganization Commission, 1989). As Kidwell and Gottlober (1991) point out, service providers and managers often think in terms of specific programs and accountability of isolated programs rather than in terms of providing flexible new services. Professional and philosophical differences are significant barriers to integrating services. These may be internal to an agency (psychologists operate one way, social workers another), or external (the schools handle problem youth differently than juvenile probation) (Kidwell and Gottlober, 1991). Agency cooperation is often hampered by conflicting eligibility requirements, rigid funding mechanisms, and staff who try to protect funding (National Commission on Children, 1991). Agencies with quite divergent professional orientations and institutional mandates are unlikely to cooperate. In times of scarce resources they are, in fact, likely to compete. In addition, they are likely to concentrate on what they can provide rather than what clients need, and hence, are unlikely to discover unmet needs and work with other agencies to fill these gaps (Melaville and Blank, 1991). Legitimate differences among agencies in philosophy and approach can lead to "turf wars." This often results in more attention being devoted to what a given agency can provide than on what the client actually needs. Hence, disagreements among agencies are exacerbated and the collective focus on meeting all of the needs of the client is diluted (Ashcroft, 1991).

At the level of the individual service provider, professionalism and specialization can work against services integration in several ways. First, professionals with specialized training tend to focus on those isolated problems they are trained to handle. They see the client through a narrow disciplinary lens (National Commission on Children, 1991). Second, existing agency staff often represent only a small part of the professional talent necessary to develop and implement a plan to deal with the multiple problems of many clients (Melaville and Blank, 1991). They often are not aware of services available through other specialized areas. Third, services integration often requires a redefinition of professionalism. Services that are required by clients may be simple, mundane activities not normally considered a part of the professional response (e.g., providing transportation). Or, services may be required in nontraditional settings or at nontraditional times that do not fit the usual definition of professionalism. Service providers are often reluctant to provide services based on the needs of clients, preferring instead to provide them based on demands and boundaries set by "professionalism" (Schorr and Schorr, 1989).

Carefully contrived and thoughtfully constructed methods won't guarantee help for a client from another agency. Cooperation among agencies isn't expected. Recently, I worked with a young man and his family. We were able to use an array of human services. A local juvenile police officer, a district probation officer, a detention home, a court psychologist, a family-service agency, a public defender, and two foster homes were involved. The case required patience and personal contacts. Despite all this, no magic happened. The young man's family, and many who had contact with him, felt frustrated. The client does not yet resemble the community's model of a "good" person. He has not yet found his way. He is still exploring himself and the world around him. He will continue to change and grow in ways that are natural for him.

It is human to feel frustration when well-intended efforts don't seem to make a difference. Helping is hard work. When you know you have made a difference in a client's life, you feel fulfilled. When bureaucracy has gotten in the way of your help, you feel frustrated.

Successful services integration efforts have been based on seven principles:

1. Comprehensive and integrated services delivery is possible only when communities move beyond cooperation to a genuinely collaborative venture at both the service delivery and system level.

2. Services integration efforts that seek major institutional reform should be initiated selectively, if at all.

3. A central authority is necessary.

4. Supplemental funding sources need authority and flexibility.

5. Initial goals should be characterized by low risk and high visibility.

6. The cultivation and maintenance of networks is vital.

7. Assessment, evaluation, and review must be part of the integrated effort.

As a new staff member, you are not in a position to lead such an effort. You are in a position to support such services integration by expanding and using your networks to serve your clients.

Summary

Very few agencies can provide all the services many clients need. You will probably work with a number of organizations; this experience may cause you to reevaluate your harsh judgment of your own organization. The formal referral process seldom works well. Agencies have differing goals and procedures. Often, many agencies compete for the same pot of tax money. Some agencies compete with one another for the same "turf."

Personal networks between the staff members of various agencies are usually more effective for referral than the formal systems. Such networks are developed over time and are based on reciprocity. Established employees may be reluctant to share their network with newcomers.

Discussion Questions

1. What are the general guidelines for deciding when and how to make referrals?

2. Describe your personal network on the job or in school. Whom do you know that can help you get things done?

References

Ashcroft, J. 1991. *Stronger Families for a Strong Missouri*. State of Missouri.

Chamberlin, L. J. 1984. *Coping With Today's Kids*. Springfield, IL: Charles C. Thomas.

Goffman, E. *Asylums*. 1961. New York: Doubleday.

Kidwell, K. D., and Gottlober, P. A. 1991. Services Integration for Families and Children in Crisis. Office of Inspector General, Department of Health and Human Services, San Francisco, CA. January.

Lefton, M., and Rosengren, W. R. 1966. Organizations and clients: Lateral and longitudinal dimensions. *American Sociological Review* 31(6), 802-10.

Melaville, A. I., and Blank, M. R. 1991. What it takes: Structuring interagency partnerships to connect children and families with comprehensive services. *Education and Human Services Consortium*. Washington, D.C. January.

National Commission on Children. 1991. Beyond Rhetoric: A New American Agenda for Children and Families. U.S. Government Printing Office, Washington, D.C.

Schorr, L. B., and Schorr, D. 1989. *Within Our Reach*. Doubleday. New York.

Smith, L. M., and Geoffrey, W. 1968. *The Complexities of an Urban Classroom: An Analysis Toward a General Theory of Teaching*. New York: Holt, Rinehart & Winston.

State Reorganization Commission, 1989. Services Integration Pilot Projects: An Evaluative Report From Arizona, Florida, Maine, Oklahoma, South Carolina. Columbia, SC. September.

Yessian, M. R., and Kvaal, M. B. 1991. Services Integration: A Twenty-Year Retrospective. Office of Inspector General, Department of Health and Human Services, Boston, MA. January.

7 Helplessness and Hope

At times, your job as a human-service worker may seem to be part of a sham. You are unable to deal with real problems. You're busy using bandages, instead of miracle drugs—treating symptoms, not causes. Others have shared this feeling of helplessness.

A child is referred to an agency for truancy. The immediate goal of the system is to return the child to school; however, the problem involves more than truancy:

> You're supposed to change something that's been going on for years and years and years. You're expected to do an impossible task. I remember a black caseworker who was dealing with an extremely hostile white kid. This caseworker told me, "I can't talk to this girl. She spits in my face. She's got to be in school. She just can't run in the streets, because somebody's going to get my ass if this kid isn't in school." I went down and talked to this girl. It was pretty obvious that she was in no condition to be in school. It was taking all her energy just to survive in her household. All the things school demands in terms of being able to put aside other problems and being able to know yourself, to accept yourself well enough to do the work you needed to do and not feeling so vulnerable to the other kids was beyond her. I talked to her. I met her family and met her sister. I spent several hours with her and went back to the office and said, "You know, this kid needs a lot of work, and she's not going to make it in school right now," and the caseworker couldn't hear that. "But she's got to be in school; she's got to do something. She's either in school or she's got to work."

A nurse working in a public health program had accepted another position. She felt that this would provide her an opportunity to suggest to her current supervisor some things that would improve the services to their clients. She began her discussion in a very quiet tone of voice and told the supervisor that she had not come to criticize any employees, but rather to make some suggestions. She tells what happened:

> Before I left, I thought, well, this is my time when I can go tell the director of nurses about this stuff. Because we had this Medicheck [federally funded] program, and you were supposed to do certain things like get urinalysis and all this at certain times of the visit, and get the sickle cell, and get hemoglobin. They weren't making an attempt to get urinalysis, and I'd really get frustrated, because we wouldn't get our money from Medicheck. One thing that had to be on this Medicheck was just simple height and weight. We got out there [to the clinic] and there wasn't a scale, and there wasn't a tape measure. So we got none of the reimbursement. I was just floored at what she told me. She acted like I should just forget it.

A worker in a mental hospital was responsible for a ward of ambulatory children who had not been outside for more than two weeks, even though the weather had been beautiful. He went to the supervisor in charge and offered to stay late after his shift was over to take the children out three afternoons per week for about an hour. The supervisor in this situation had a very real problem. She told him that she couldn't let him do that, because "We can't pay you overtime, and the hospital insurance would not cover you if anything happened to the children when you were outside with them." The hospital worker then went one step further up the administrative ladder. He puts it this way:

> I really started protesting about the kids not being taken outside, and I wanted to work with them, so they started getting even with me by pulling me from one ward to another — making me distribute tables to the hospital, that sort of thing, sending me to a ward with geriatrics where there's no real need for psychiatric aides, where I'd have to be changing bed sheets and stuff like that.

Sometimes unpredictable circumstances can improve client services. An institutional nurse took advantage of a change in administrators to deliver health care to her clients, in spite of the rules and regulations of the organization:

> For the first six years that I worked there, it was literally impossible to get a boy a pair of glasses. 'We don't do that here.

Our budget isn't set up for that.' And about four years ago, we got a new superintendent and a new clinic director. I went downtown, talked to several optometrists, and got together with one of them. He gave us a fine, fair price on refracting the boys with visual problems. I went to the new clinic director and told him that six boys a month would be going, possibly eight at times, for refraction. And I just sort of included it as part of our format, and he said, 'Oh, you provide glasses here,' and I said, 'We've always done it that way.' So, for four years now the boys with visual problems have been getting glasses. I've never been called on it. If I ever am, I'll just say, 'Well, we've always done it that way.'

Though you might think that this nurse's methods are deceptive, dishonest, and unethical, you can't help but appreciate the fact that the clients were better served. There will likely be a time in your career when you'll have to make the same kind of difficult decision. The nurse describes her methods this way:

We get boys that are blind in one eye since birth and nobody knows why. We get boys that have huge hernias. We have boys with torn knee cartilages and just a myriad of ailments. Well, our chief resource is _____ Hospital, which is also a state facility, and, by reciprocal arrangements, we're supposed to be able to get services from them. It's much easier said than done. They want you to write a letter and send a full history, and then they'll write back to you and let you know when the boy can have an appointment.

When I first started to work there, it took upwards of four months sometimes to get an appointment for a boy. So I came to the conclusion that there had to be a better way. Now, when I get a boy who needs further care and needs it this week, not in three or four months, I do kind of a sneaky thing. I send them straight up to the hospital with a guard and a signed consent form that enables the hospital to treat them and send them straight to a patient screening clinic. This is where the people from the street walk in. I've gotten quite a few phone calls and a reprimand here and there from people at the hospital for doing that; but, that way, that kid is seen that day, and he has an appointment within the next five days to return for treatment. This saves a lot of time, and it saves a lot of stress and worry on the kids' part, and it probably doesn't really put the hospital off that much, because I've been doing it for years now.

If there's something that's not an emergency — doesn't need to be looked at right away — and they (our administrators) have no plans for transferring that boy immediately, then I go through legitimate channels.

A white female social worker assigned to a black community by a state agency was having trouble relating to her clients, but then she found a "nonpolicy" way to better help them with their problems:

> We found that some of our clients were remarkably well-put-together people, and they could help other clients, so we had clients helping other clients and doing things with them. We had a lot of teenagers working for us as volunteers. Sometimes, a particular child of mine would be having problems, and I'd know that a certain one of the volunteer kids who was really in close contact with us in the office had had a similar problem and had worked it through, and I'd say, "Would you talk to so-and-so?" And it built the volunteer's self-esteem to be able to do this, and yet also he got through to the child where I couldn't have.

In these last two examples, the nurse and the social worker brought about change on their own. Next, an English teacher describes a group effort to make change:

> Nothing is so important to a teacher as his textbook. This Bible of the classroom, this expounder of all knowledge, is sacred as Holy Writ itself, and heaven help those pagans who fail to be guided by its pervasive knowledge. As might be expected, I had not fully realized this when I volunteered with sophomorish zeal to be on the committee to revise the textbook for freshman classes. After having experimented for one year with one freshman class without a textbook, I was to report to the group of teachers on how well the experiment went. After having completed this assignment, two of my English cohorts and I were to meet with the corresponding committee members from our sister school and make recommendations about texts. This we dutifully did. The attack on our recommendations came at the next department meeting.

> Two veterans of thirty years' teaching had rallied their anti-new-textbooks associates and quickly made a frontal assault. They stormed the committee members with poignant questions, like 'Why should this textbook be changed?' 'What do these new books have that this book doesn't?' 'Children are basically the same, so why change textbooks?' 'A good story is timeless, isn't it?' Finally, they struck with their atomic question: 'Have we voted on this change of textbook?'

> They obviously had those recommending and favoring the adoption of a new textbook on the horns of a dilemma. For what true flag-carrying American could deny this privilege, this remnant of our democracy? The vote was taken, and the

anti-new-textbook confederation had won. The committee members slid out of the room in a cloud of disgrace. My faith in the liberality of English teachers had been shaken. Where were the Deweys of yesteryear?

The war, however, was not over. Several teachers who were not present at the field of battle had not yet voted. When the absentee vote was counted, the conflict was stalemated: 11 yes, 11 no. Of course, the fortunes of war are fickle. The anti-new-textbook forces had had their moment in the sun. The returns from our sister school on the eastern front were nearly unanimous for the adoption of new freshman textbooks. And so, the battle of the books ended, and only a few remnants (an occasional snide comment, scornful glance, or uncomfortable silence) attested to the ferocity and intensity of this monumental war.

This description of a department's struggle to change one textbook illustrates the difficulty involved in bringing about change in an institution. Interdepartmental, intradepartmental, and administration/departmental problems are interwoven. Groups form. Traditionalists believe that those who want change are moving too swiftly, whereas enthusiasts assume that traditionalists will never change.

You may want to improve conditions and methods. You may want to effect changes. You may confront unresolved job conflicts. These unresolved conflicts can be frustrating and can produce a general feeling of tension. Supervisors will perceive this tension—some sooner than others. Your supervisors' reactions to your state depend on a variety of factors, including their mental health and their general attitudes and behavior toward employees. Their attitudes may range from "Let 'em bitch" to "I wonder what's wrong?" Their behavior may range from denial of problems to friendly counseling sessions to promotion. If you are a valued employee, if your tension hasn't become destructive, if an opening exists, you may be promoted.

Burnout: Its Treatment and Control

There is usually great anticipation when students complete their education and begin their first jobs as human-service workers. Edelwich and Brodsky (1980) describe many of the newcomers' expectations that frequently go unfulfilled. These include unrealistic expectations of clients' roles and attitudes; the expectation that the individual can perform miracles showing immediate or universal success; and the expectation that the job will provide appreciation, rewarding experiences, chance for training, advancement, status, and simple solutions to any problems that may occur. The original enthusiasm can turn to frustration when reality sets in.

Job-related anxiety and unhappiness can affect not only your job, but also the other areas of your life—if you allow it to do so. Your temper is quicker, your patience is shorter, your tolerance lower. Increased stress can lead to physical illness. When frustration reaches the point at which you can't stand it, you must do something. A carefully kept journal of the sort described in Chapter 2 can be of great help. By going back a few months and reading your entries, you may be able to understand how you developed the feelings you now experience. As you read what you wrote, look for significant events and people, as well as your reactions to them. Is there a pattern? What made you feel good? What made you feel bad? Can you change the way in which you spend your time on the job to get more of the good feelings and fewer of the bad feelings?

Your socialization coach may be someone within the system to whom you can go when you feel frustrated. When people who know you outside the job begin to ask, "What's wrong?" it might be a good idea to tell them. Your spouse or roommate may assume that your unhappiness is being caused by them. By discussing the job situation with them, you let them know that it's not their fault, and you give yourself a chance to hear the words that describe your frustration. Your journal and your conversations may provide temporary relief. With some of the tension reduced, you may be able to think more clearly. Don't force yourself to choose between living with things as they are and quitting. When you're burned out, the choice may seem that simple, but it's more complex than that. For example, there are many ways of staying and many ways of quitting.

You can quit simply by not showing up, and you will soon be fired. You can go to work and make enough mistakes that you get fired. You can sacrifice your job in a once-and-for-all showdown with the boss, in the hope that it will lead to improvements after you're gone. Let's assume that you have decided to stay and deal with burnout. The following examples may reflect your feelings. Perhaps the reactions of these new employees will be of help to you (some of these anecdotes were used earlier in a different context):

> Then, the frustration of not being able to make progress became overwhelming. Everything I started became bogged down with paperwork, policies, and apathetic coworkers. It soon occurred

to me that attempting to change the entire setup was unrealistic. So, I began to single out specific residents with specific problems and concentrated my efforts on them. By channeling my efforts on one resident at a time, I could actually see some positive results over a period of time. When one child learned to walk alone, or learned to feed himself, or was placed in a home setting, all the hassle was worthwhile.

A shift in focus from the larger organization and its problems to the individual client gave this employee temporary relief from the sense of being overwhelmed. This worked for her. For others, an emphasis on individual clients has been the primary cause of burnout.

The first six months that I worked in this rural mental-health clinic, I felt so good when one of my people called me at home. It was kind of a high I got. I had really communicated caring and concern. They'd always apologize (for calling me at home), but I'd listen without showing any impatience. Once, even I called the supervising psychiatrist at home and got her to phone in a new prescription for this one client. It turned out that the client was really a drug-dependent person and had been using both our agencies and two local G.P.'s to supply drugs for the habit.

Pretty soon, I liked the phone calls at home less and less. I began to distrust clients, and this distrust got communicated, I'm sure. My whole life was dependent on the success of my clients and the quality of my relationship with them.

It has taken me more than two years to realize that a lot of my job is to help people change their values, beliefs, and behaviors. This process takes a long time. Deception is a way of life for a lot of my clients. It's not directed at me personally. People grow and change at different rates. It seems that some of them I can't help at all. Before I came to accept these things, I went so far as to get an unlisted [telephone] number. Now I just do the best I can, and that's good. I have a job, but that job is not my life. My professional self is still related to my personal self, but not nearly so much. I feel a lot better this way.

A similar conclusion was drawn by a first-year English teacher who was having a lot of trouble getting her students interested in composition.

I thought it might be interesting to try to start a newspaper. I brought this idea up to a couple of other teachers. "You have got to be kidding. You can't do that. Your class will get too loud. How are you going to teach gerunds and participles if you are going to print a newspaper?" Right away, I learned to keep my mouth closed and to go ahead and do something if I wanted to do it, without telling anybody.

After what I've been through, I came to the conclusion that you have to find the strength within yourself to survive these things. You've got to come to grips with them and decide what's important to you and for whom you are working. I was terrified, depressed, and disillusioned for the first year, and am still disillusioned now. At least I know what's real, and I know I have made my choice. All I have to do is carry through. As long as you're happy with yourself, you can tolerate what's around and above you.

The attitudes of your coworkers may support your feelings of despair and frustration. Established employees who come across as cruel, indifferent, and incompetent may have been burned out as a result of a series of events. They seem not to care. Perhaps they were dedicated staff members and helpful supervisors; now they passively accept what has become a norm for them. They may be resigned to accepting things as they are. Accepting things as they are doesn't have to mean accepting things as unchanging.

"Human-service workers need to set limits for themselves. They need to become aware of their own warning signals of fatigue or extreme frustration, stopping themselves before they burn out. Through eagerness and concern for others, many human-service workers are careless about the extra hours they put into their work. Ultimately we serve our clients best if we pace ourselves and do not neglect our own support network of friends and family" (Mandell and Schram, 1985:130).

One of the better works on burnout is by Christina Maslach and is referenced at the end of this chapter. A few of the essential ideas will be summarized here. One of the first traps we fall into is asking "*Who* is to blame for burnout?" "*Who's* responsible; *who* caused this to happen?" Of course, what we get back is a *who* answer. Posing the question differently:"*What* is causing burnout?" provides a different answer. Rather than looking for defective people, our attention is focused on the situation in which we find ourselves. Simply put, burnout is best understood and dealt with in terms of situational sources of job-related, interpersonal stress.

Most people interpret burnout as reflecting some basic personality defect. They feel something is wrong with them — they are too weak or incompetent or have become a bad person. This, of course, is in response to the *who* question. One other response to the *who* question is putting the blame on the other guy. "My students don't appreciate me." "My clients are defective."

We get into the habit of blaming the victim. We begin to see our students and clients in negative terms. We see the recipients of our help as people with problems. For example, the AIDS epidemic has been socially defined as a disease of already marginalized groups. Thus the stigma attached to AIDS as an illness is layered upon pre-existing stigma. Working with such clients, therefore, is going to require sensitivity to the magnification of other issues caused by the social stigma. As the AIDS epidemic continues, more and more human-service workers — in education, health care, social welfare, and law enforcement — work with clients who are infected with the HIV virus. You will be confronted with a set of issues that result not only from the medical disease, but to the stigma associated with it. This stigma ranges from William Buckley, Jr.'s suggestion that everyone detected with AIDS should be tattooed in the upper forearm . . . to coworkers who tell you not to let the HIV positive people sneeze on you. AIDS probably would have been stigmatized to some extent regardless of whom it infected, but through an accident, AIDS in the United States has been largely a disease of already stigmatized groups. Most adults in this country diagnosed with AIDS are homosexual men and intravenous drug abusers. Additionally, blacks and Hispanics are disproportionately represented.

It takes effort to kick this habit of blaming the victim — and clients don't make it easy. They may be indifferent or downright hostile to our attempt to help them. Added to this is the lack of positive feedback. We hear complaints and criticisms from them. With this comes an increasing level of emotional stress. The possibility of change or improvement seems more distant. These other people are the *who* that are causing our problem.

When one asks *what* is causing the burnout, a different set of responses is available. Burnout is high when you lack a sense of control over the help you are providing. You have been taught how to do your job. You know how to help. You know what constitutes good teaching, good counseling, good social work, good nursing. Yet, the situation controls what you can do. Having to teach a report-card-driven curriculum is an extreme, but not hypothetical, example. The principal insists that you teach a kindergarten curriculum so that you will be able to fill out the report card to make the parents happy. This lack of autonomy and loss of control over the outcome of your job adds much to your emotional strain.

Helpers can be trapped in their roles by institutional rules. Such rules will often force you to operate in situations that are difficult. If your job does not allow you to take temporary breaks from stressful contacts with clients and students, you may feel trapped.

You are on the spot with no one else to share the work or to help. This out-of-control feeling adds to the emotional strain.

As we discussed earlier, your coworkers may be one element in a situation that produces burnout. Problems in relating to your peers can contribute to burnout in two ways. First, they can be a direct source of emotional stress adding to your feelings of emotional exhaustion. Second, they can rob you of a very valuable resource when coping with problems similar to yours. Some work environments appear designed to promote conflict rather than cooperation. Competition for favored positions, promotions, and other forms of recognition can create one-upmanship, backbiting, and put-downs.

Another answer to the *what* question can be supervisors. As with coworkers, if your dealings with supervisors are unsatisfactory, the resulting tension and friction add to your overload. A mismatch of expectations can easily create mutual misunderstandings and animosity. Your supervisors are also under pressure. They are responsible for seeing that the plans, policies, and procedures of your organization are carried out. Your supervisors are the ones who define the constraints of your job—in other words, what constitutes successful service. Whether it be to cure illness, enlighten ignorance, or to help people relieve stress—the institution is mobilized to achieve an abstract goal. You also are oriented toward that goal, but sometimes your method of achieving it will clash with the organization's procedures and your supervisors' ideas of the best methods.

Maslach (1986) dedicates several chapters to handling burnout. Her coping techniques are described at three different levels— individual, social, and institutional. Some people learn to work *smarter* instead of working harder. They make changes in the way they handle their job so they are less stressed and more efficient. Working smarter means setting realistic goals without knocking the impossible dream and letting go of noble ideals. Sometimes we can do the same things differently. Not only can major tasks be done differently, such as changing your instructional methods, but everyday tasks might be handled in new ways. Perhaps you don't intend to change your teaching style, but you might consider changing the way you begin and end your classes. Intermittent breaks or rest periods allow for emotional breathers. Reducing your appointments from thirty to twenty-five minutes allows you to close the door and take a couple of deep breaths. Take things less personally and try to make the situation more objective. A shift from "their pain is my pain" to "their pain is their pain" can sometimes help. Accentuate the positive.

Those of us who work with people sometimes get to the point where we focus on what is wrong and forget what is right. Earlier, the idea of keeping a personal log was suggested. Maslach calls this "know thyself" and describes a daily stress and tension log. Such self-observation may be the beginning of self-understanding. It is also essential to find time for rest and relaxation. One person may choose meditation, another biofeedback, others walk, read the daily paper, take a hot bath, or view television. Making the transition from work to home where you have your own life, can sometimes take time.

Social support can come from positive companionship with colleagues. Establishing good relationships with colleagues can provide comfort, perhaps insight into a difficult case, and a sounding board for your feelings, activities, successes, and failures. If you are fortunate enough to have coworkers with a good sense of humor, you may find that shared laughter is a pleasant, temporary escape from the rigors of your job.

Sometimes changes can be made in the work place itself. Such changes usually require the cooperation of others. Work which is especially stressful might be divided. Nurses working with dying patients, teachers with behaviorally impaired students, prison guards with particularly difficult cell blocks might often be relieved by an agreed-upon rotation. At least you would be able to look forward to a brief respite from a particularly stressful situation.

So You Want to Change the Organization

What can you as an individual do, and how should you go about attempting to change those practices and policies that, in your judgment, need to be altered? There is a wide range of positions that can be taken. One position addresses the basic institutions themselves. Adherents of this position seek to rearrange the structure and roots of power. They would free the institutions from what they see as wornout bureaucratic structures, political associations, and social-class influences. For example, they would redistribute income rather than provide specialized government programs for housing, health, and education.

At the other extreme, the concept of change does not address institutions; instead, it focuses on individuals in an effort to help them to cope. Simply put, the focus is on the preparation of each individual to effectively deal with the bureaucratic institutions that deliver services. Such a position focuses on the development of skills and competencies that are needed to overcome the bureaucratic institution's shortcomings. Adherents of this position hold that those of us who develop and practice these skills at the highest level will be the most successful members of our society.

These positions regarding institutional change could place every human-service practitioner in a dilemma—the need to choose one or the other. Even if one assumes that these two alternatives—either revolutionizing the institutional structures or focusing on the development of individuals—are of equal value, neither offers much hope to the practitioner. The hard reality is that there are no equal alternatives. Our society is not on the brink of a revolution; it seems that a total and systematic forward-looking change is not going to occur in the near future. If such a revolution were to occur, it would undoubtedly be more effectively carried out by the masses of youthful nonprofessionals rather than by the professional human-service practitioners.

For us, there is another option—an intermediate level of social change and direct practice that focuses on both the individual and the institution. I suggest this middle position for those of you who are attempting to survive as well as service your client populations. I believe that the practitioner must recognize basic social problems as well as the criticisms appropriately made about the direct practice of help giving. Action through practice to deal with institutional dysfunction while improving service to clients is the challenge we all face. This challenge will test your ability to maintain a balance between your technical competence, your psychological health, and your ability to step away and see the larger picture.

Your decision to be a human-service worker implies an acceptance of your clients' immediate problems and their concern with their environments. You have been trained to understand the strains (social, economic, physiological, and psychological) with which clients must cope. The awareness of these realities must be tempered by a continued awareness of the environment in which the bureaucracy places you.

Ready or not, you are expected to be a help giver and a bureaucrat. To state the issue directly, you have technical competencies and skills, but you are probably unprepared for organizational life. You need bureaucratic skills in order to capitalize on the possibility for organizational change as well as to neutralize stresses and strains that will be placed on you. An understanding of the bureaucratic process will provide an opportunity for self-direction. The acquisition of bureaucratic skills may lead to greater satisfaction on the job as well as higher levels of professional accomplishment.

It is unproductive to think of bureaucracy as bad, as something to be overcome. Bureaucracy can be understood as a complex environment in which purposes are pursued. Often, these purposes are blurred, as each member of the bureaucracy privately pursues the goals that are most important to him or her. The bureaucratic environment can be so confusing to the newcomer that he or she simply becomes debilitated. As you look at the established staff in your group, you see individuals who have followed the path of least resistance. The help-giving bureaucrat who is satisfied with the status quo is not uncommon. For those who are not satisfied — those who hold visions of what their organizations might be — discretion and research are vital resources.

First, you should research your relationship with your supervisor, specifically focusing on the content of your job as it is viewed by that supervisor. Your supervisor will have some conception of the job that you are expected to perform. Although the specifications of your job may be partly determined by organizational rules derived from a statutory base, they were most likely established by one or more previous job holders — one of whom may have been your supervisor. Once you are clearly aware of the supervisor's view of your job, you can begin to estimate where he or she might be in terms of anticipating the kinds of arguments that will be presented to you during any future disagreements.

Many opportunities to initiate progress are open only to those who work within the system. By listening and observing, you will gain opportunities to help move your organization in the desired direction. All organizations change:

> Sometimes organizations change because they want to, but more basically, they do so because they cannot avoid it. For any given bureaucrat, the kind of changes he or she wants may not have occurred; or they may occur too slowly; or the individual may feel that she or he plays no part in the process; or for many reasons, the individual may be discouraged about it or oblivious to it. But none of this alters the fact that the forces and pressures that produce change are at play in organizations at least as powerfully and persistently as are those that promote stability. A crude but fair test of this proposition is the difficulty that anyone would have in identifying even a single organization that is today precisely as it was even a year or two ago. No such organization exists or ever will. The conventional wisdom on the subject, which implies that bureaucracy, unlike everything else in this world, has somehow immunized itself against change, is simply incorrect.

Organizational change is a continuous process rather than a sporadic event; everything [sic] affects everything. Things are always happening that make it easier to press certain initiatives and harder to press others: a staff member quits, and so some clique or alliance is strengthened or weakened; the organization moves to another building with a different layout of office space, so the director casually observes one unit more often and another less often while heading for lunch each day; the budget is reduced, held the same, or enlarged, inducing some to throw up their hands in disgust and others to compete more aggressively for everything in sight; one kind of client problem appears less frequently and another more frequently. Each of these events upsets the equilibrium of the system to some degree, making it more internally fluid than it was before. The bureaucrat who is sensitive to these things and can think a few moves ahead is the one who is most likely to see that some greater or lesser nuance in the organization's evolution occurs because he or she willed it. Though change is the most continuous organizational process, the responsibility to bring it about is part of no individual job description (Baer and Federico, 1978).[1]

Effective change comes neither in large chunks nor as a result of showdowns and other dramatic occurrences. Rather, it is an almost daily process of small adjustments, each of which makes succeeding adjustments more or less likely to occur. The combination of these changes shapes the organization. With skill, careful planning, and good research, effective change will come in small quiet increments and will be produced through persistent action based on careful observation of your organization.

Unless your research tells you otherwise, your supervisor is probably the first one you should talk to if you want to instigate any changes in the way things are done. Before you make the approach, consider this: you must be far enough into your present job to be fully socialized, yet far enough away from your next job to be fully involved in your present position. If you are too close to your next job, you may be seen as a "lame duck." Now, if you've decided to go ahead, lay out the problems you have seen and ask for advice and counsel. This will make your supervisor feel helpful; moreover, your supervisor may have a good idea regarding the problems you've come to discuss.

It is difficult to make real changes in an organization. There are many theories regarding organizational change. These theories

---

[1] Reprinted with permission from *Educating the Baccalaureate Social Worker,* Volume 1, Copyright 1978, Ballinger Publishing Company.

range from Golden's (1990) "Innovations by Groping Along" to French and Bell's (1990) eclectic approach to organizational change. Both of these sources provide a conceptual framework that serious readers may find helpful in avoiding some mistakes as they try to change organizations. Don't expect any pat answers in any of the literature.

Often, attempts to effect changes in organizations fail because the attempts are sucked into the system. Social-welfare agencies and health-care agencies try to coordinate services for multiproblem families through team approaches, interagency case conferences, and new legislation. At times, attempted changes are treated as experiments or demonstrations. The special status of innovation threatens the life of the attempted change. First, the new program is given its own special budget. Second, the originators are pleased when the boss proudly points the program out to visiting dignitaries and mentions it in the annual report; however, once the program has lost its public relations value, the special budget on which it has become dependent may well disappear.

Often, organizational change attempts, or innovative programs, are isolated from the larger system. "It and the rest of the system become rigid separately, in defense against one another" (Lynton, 1969:400). The isolation produces a win-or-lose situation, a battle between the new and the old. The old "has a crust of traditional practices which nothing short of dynamite can remove" (Levy and Herzog, 1971:199). Usually, the old controls a loyal army.

Now for some hope—organizations do change. Why do they change? Or, more important to you, how can they be changed? The most honest answer to these questions is that nobody really knows, but we have begun to find some answers. In her book *Within Our Reach: Breaking the Cycle of Disadvantage*, Lisbeth Schorr (1989) provides a direction for change in human services programming. According to Schorr, successful programs for children offer a broad spectrum of services; cross traditional professional and bureaucratic boundaries; see the child in the context of family and the family in the context of its surroundings; employ staff who are perceived by those they serve as people who care about them and respect them, people they can trust; and who find ways to adapt or circumvent traditional professional and bureaucratic limitations when necessary to meet the needs of those they serve. Some of the major conditions for promoting and sustaining change, or organizational innovations, are discussed in the next section.

Some Conditions That Facilitate Change

Melaville and Blank (1991) summarize the five conditions they judge necessary to produce change in the human services sector.

1. *Environment*—The most supportive environment for dealing with problems is one in which identifying and implementing the solution is a top priority of key decision makers, service providers, and the community.

2. *Resources*—Resources of all kinds must be pooled and reconfigured to achieve hoped for results.

3. *Policies*—Included in these are federal, state, and local-level policies, guidelines, and definitions that establish mandates, target populations, eligibility requirements, and so on.

4. *People*—The people who lead, participate in, and eventually implement change are central to a successful program.

5. *Process*—A successful program includes establishing a communication and problem-solving process to make decisions, agree on roles, and resolve conflicts.

But before you start to change things, ask your immediate supervisor for help. The answer to your request may indicate how he or she would react to your direct suggestions. In the process of giving you help, your supervisor may think of the idea that you had. There are few things more powerful than a boss with an idea that he or she thinks may work. One staff member put it this way: "I'd kept the idea up in the minds of the administrators and all of a sudden they thought it was a great idea." In other words, "those who had power, sanctions, and communication linkages and boundary roles appeared to be important in the adoption of innovations" (Baldridge and Burnham, 1975:175). This means that those who control resources, rewards, punishments, and contacts are more likely to bring about change than those who don't have such control.

Although you may feel better after you've complained to the boss about a particular problem, complaining won't solve the problem, and it probably won't help the boss feel better. Before you present a problem to your supervisor, draw up a list of possible solutions. You should order your solutions, beginning with the best one and ending with the one that you like the least.

There may be times when you feel that you need to go around rules and regulations—to skip some links in the chain of command. Devito (1974), a psychiatrist turned hospital administrator, says that such behavior is probably a symptom of organizational anxiety. As an administrator, he would react in a rather neutral way if you went directly to him with a suggestion or a complaint. At least he would not punish you for making an appointment. Not all administrators feel this way. When you can't get what you think you ought to have from your immediate superiors, you need to ask yourself this question: "Will going around them to get what I want be worth the price I may have to pay?" Even if you win this time and get what you want, what about tomorrow?

If you decide to go around your immediate superiors, tell them that you are going to see their boss. (If you ask for their permission, they may refuse.) When you have chosen to tell your supervisors that you're going to see the boss, don't expect the next person up the line to support you or to be pleased to see you. Your visit indicates that something is amiss. Waves may be coming. The status quo is being threatened. If your immediate supervisor insists on going with you to see the boss, the boss probably won't support your position in your supervisor's presence; organizational morale depends on the boss's support of your supervisor. If the big boss believes that you are right, your supervisor may get chewed out after you leave. Even if your immediate supervisor is not present when you talk to the boss, it is very likely that the boss has already been briefed in advance on the issue and been presented with the arguments you have used unsuccessfully with your supervisor. Therefore, you should be prepared to present new and stronger arguments. Continued appeal to higher authority usually follows a particular process—your arguments are conveyed to the next in command before you arrive. It can be a tough road. Be careful. Gather as much information as possible about the people and the issues involved.

An experienced security officer in an institution for delinquents has this advice: "If you feel you've got to do it, make sure what you're trying to do is important enough. You have to use good judgment and common sense when you decide to buck the system." You should remember that: (1) all of the details need to be worked out ahead of time; (2) if you don't follow up every detail, your efforts are likely to fail; (3) many of the people with whom you will deal mean well but don't really know what they are doing, or why; and (4) you probably haven't thought of the best answer, so keep asking yourself the question.

When you go to see your supervisor, or when your supervisor comes to you, don't cover too much ground. Don't try to cure the ills of the world with one program change. Simply put, don't bring up irrelevant issues. Keep your personal beliefs to yourself. Deal only with issues that are directly related to the change that you want to discuss. International politics and religious beliefs probably don't have anything to do with it.

One alternative to the direct approach is the "everything is ready to go" approach. You have thought out all of the possible problems that will be created by the change you want to make. You have at least one solution for each of the problems. The budget will not be hurt. Other staff members' turf has been protected or negotiated. Other agencies and organizations have informally agreed to your proposal. The professional literature, including newsletters, journals, and recent books, indicates that your proposed change is a good idea. The change will help the clients. The risk is small. The change will be a feather in the boss's cap. This strategy involves time and the help of other people. The majority of these other people will mean well and intend to keep their commitment to you when the chips are down, but some may not. It is a good idea to be two deep. Each necessary element in your plan should have at least one alternative, in case somebody backs out or something goes wrong. Planning, coordination, and constant follow-up are key factors in this approach to change. Putting together such a package will require time beyond your normal working hours. The wrapping on this ready-to-go package is the potential benefit to the image of your organization and its leaders.

An example of an "everything is ready to go" strategy is provided by the vocational training program developed by a youth supervisor in a correctional institution. He modified the strategy by using a stepwise approach. The key elements in his package included the following: no financial cost, negotiated turf, a potentially therapeutic program for clients, more efficient utilization of staff skills, an agreement with major unions, tax-deductible contributions from community businesses, and a lot of patience.

> One of the things that I felt was badly needed out there at the institution was a program that a kid could get into that would do him some good when he got back out on the street. A lot of kids liked mechanical work—things they could do with their hands. They didn't need a lot of books, because a lot of those kids couldn't read. They can't use figures too well.

> I felt that small engine mechanical repair work must be a place to begin. I was told that it couldn't be done, because we didn't have the equipment, money to buy the equipment, or a qualified teacher. So it was just kind of sloughed off.

> Well, I still felt that the program was worthwhile. I believed in it, so I kept at it—still getting the same answers, until one day I got a little disgusted with the whole thing, and I decided that

I would get equipment some place, and I would teach it myself. I had been an auto mechanic for about twenty years, so I went downtown to [a retail chain store] and I talked to the manager. I explained to him what I had in mind and that we needed tools to be able to do the work. He told me he would check it out with his superiors and let me know in a couple of weeks. Two weeks went by and, sure enough, they came out with a nice set of tools for us. That was a big step, and then they also threw in five or six small engines. So I went back to the institution with it and said, 'Now I've got the tools, I have the engines to work on. Now let's see if we can't get this set up.' They came back with, 'Well, we don't have any place to put it, no room to accommodate that kind of job program.' At that time, we had one wing in our building that we didn't operate anymore, and there were 16 rooms back in the wing. They were small rooms, but I felt that we could take and knock a wall out between two rooms and make one workshop out of it. I went up and asked the superintendent about it. He said, 'Well, can you get the boys to do it?' I said, 'They would jump at the chance to try to knock a jail down.' So he said, 'Well, you'll have to check with the union on it.' And, of course, the union said that we couldn't do it, because there would probably be supervisors or somebody around there other than the boys that would be doing the work. We had a little hassle over that, but they finally agreed that I could use boys to knock the walls down in the two rooms where I wanted to make a workshop. The boys were enthusiastic. They made a work bench, painted it, painted the cabinets, and we moved in with our tools and the cabinets. We were able to have five boys in the morning class.

Now I felt that the workshops could be expanded. We could have a wood shop. I had listened to the boys and heard a lot of boys say that they'd like to do a little wood work, and we set up a wood shop.

I had heard where manufacturers farmed out work from the company to different places to have work done. I went to a company in [a small town] and talked to the president, and he had room on an assembly line to put radar ranges together. I went back to the institution and presented the idea to the superintendent. We had boys assigned from one of the programs on an outside job which had been a failure. I was informed by the superintendent that it was against state law. It was against the law to bring work in and have boys work on it. It would be kind of like a . . . considered a sweat shop thing, I suppose. But he did call the state capitol and ask about it, and it kind of went into limbo, so I kept toying around with the idea.

I kept the idea up in their minds and up in front. Eventually, they decided that the programs were a good idea. Some of our boys now get skills, earn a salary, and have a good reason to read and work with numbers.

In one sense, the following strategy is a variation of the "everything is ready to go" approach. The big difference is that, in using this approach, you use the power of the structure in order to affect the bureaucracy. If you want to play high stakes, this is a long shot that works best in big, state-controlled organizations. In other words, "Large complex organizations with a heterogeneous environment are more likely to adopt innovations than a small, simple organization with a relatively stable, homogeneous environment" (Baldridge and Burnham, 1975:175).

After you have completed the checklist of financial costs, potential problems and corresponding solutions, other staff and agency turf, improved service to clients, and an estimate of the board's response, two additional major items must be considered before you take this approach. First, be sure that your plans do not interfere with any private profit being made by your superiors. Second, you must be able to afford clothing, food, and shelter (in case your plans don't work). This approach is similar to the "everything is ready to go" strategy, except that it involves an additional step: you need to obtain the support of the state director, the government, or the council — that is, the really big boss. (At times, the really big boss is money. A federal grant can be the equivalent of the big boss's approval.)

How can you manage to see the really big boss? Most state directors' offices are in the state capitol. Whatever you do, don't make an appointment. If you do, an administrative aide will want to know the nature of your visit in advance; this could involve your lower-level bosses. At this point, you do not want them to be involved. Find out when the state director is in, and go to his or her office. Do this on your own time. Just walk in. Tell the receptionist that you have an idea that will either improve the service to clients or reduce the agency's budget, but that you need the director's advice and counsel. Indicate that you will wait, it will only take a few minutes, and that you would be happy to see the director between scheduled appointments. At this point, you may think that this strategy won't work — "They'll never let me in!" Maybe you are right. That's one of the chances you have to take.

State directors can easily become isolated from what is going on at the grassroots level. They have most likely been away from the action for a long time. At one time, they may have been professional helpers. Within the limits of professional ethics, you are asking them to participate with another professional in formulating organizational goals (Wade, 1967). In order to participate effectively, they need to know what is going on at the grassroots level. This creates a conflict, because they don't know what's really going on, and they don't know how to find out. Your visit represents a chance for them to get out into the real world of their organizations without ever leaving their offices. They see your visit as an opportunity to visit the troops without actually going into the field.

When you are introduced to a state director, chances are the weather and other light topics will be discussed, as they are in any awkward social situation. Once you've begun to feel comfortable, get right to the point. Have your story prepared. Practice in the presence of some intelligent listeners. Don't memorize, but have a key-word outline in your head. Your entire pitch shouldn't require more than three minutes. Of course, you have to allow the director to interrupt with questions. Answer them straightforwardly, and go on to the next part of your outline. Remember, don't discuss unrelated personal beliefs that may be controversial. Listen closely for any sign of interest. Be sensitive to nonverbal messages that indicate that it's time for you to leave: if the director looks away from you, gazes at papers on the desk, or stands up, your time is up. The director shouldn't have to open the door to the office in order to indicate that it's time for you to go.

When you go home and tell your local boss that the state director thinks you have a good idea, all hell will break loose. Don't try to stop it. When your immediate supervisor calms down, it might help if you say that you told the state director that only under the guidance of a manager like yours could your proposal be carried out. Allow your superiors to have a genuine role in the planning and control of the new program as soon as possible. If they are to be committed to the program, they must feel that at least a part of the change is their idea. Also, since your superiors most likely have been around the organization longer than you have, they will be able to see problems that you have not seen, find solutions that you didn't think of, and open local doors more easily than you can. If you get this far, good luck, careful planning, and constant follow up are the keys.

One consequence of this change strategy is that some staff members at your level may be threatened and jealous: threatened, because they aren't sure how the change will affect their jobs; jealous, because they wish that they had the nerve to do what you have done. Four examples of this strategy are described in the following paragraphs.

A street-therapy program is operating under the sponsorship of a state mental-health clinic servicing a severely depressed urban area. Through the program, both professional and paraprofessional mental-health workers provide client services in homes rather than having all of the clients come to a clinic. At the time the program was initiated, it was a novel idea. All the steps listed earlier were a part of the planning of this program. The support of the state director was secured by the social worker in a manner very similar to the one described here. The local mental-health clinic and its local director have received statewide recognition and considerable support and cooperation from other help-giving agencies in the community.

Another successful application of this change strategy resulted in a new treatment program for institutionalized delinquents in direct helping roles with geriatric mental patients in a state hospital. The Associated Press and CBS devoted feature stories and television programming to the dramatic results of this program. The administrations of the institution for the delinquents and the state mental hospital received statewide awards for the program. This program change was initiated through a combination of federal grant money and visits to the state director's office.

The third example of this strategy involves the development of a halfway house for adult criminal offenders. In this case, the state director was a combination of a state supreme court judge, the state bar association, and an officer of a police chiefs' association, each of whom expressed approval to their local counterparts.

A program that was initiated by a prison psychologist who had carefully planned and even operated a small-scale drug-treatment program for inmates had negative results. The psychologist had methodically developed all of the necessary support at the local level and had gotten the state director's blessing. The program had been in operation for two months when the psychologist was invited to participate in a professional conference. Upon checking into his hotel room, he saw that there were empty whiskey bottles and lipstick-covered cigarette butts in the trash can and assumed that the room had not been cleaned.

Eventually, he suspected that perhaps this was not the case, because the rest of the room seemed to be in good order. Having worked with inmates for some time, he had become wise to the ways of the street. He began a more methodical search of the room and discovered a small bag of marijuana taped to the back of the toilet tank. He removed the bag of marijuana, took it down to the desk clerk, and asked that his room be changed. Within ten minutes, three squad cars of the local police arrived at the hotel to search the room that the psychologist had originally been given. It turned out that he had been set up because his drug-treatment program was interfering with a lieutenant and three guards who had been selling illicit drugs to inmates.

Administrative approval—support from your boss in dealing with the initial reactions of coworkers—gives you a good start in changing what you set out to change. But it's only a start. The good feelings of accomplishment and reward are luxuries to be enjoyed. Now the real work begins. To make the change work—to really help clients— could be a lifelong task. The hardest part is to get the ball rolling, especially when you have been pushing uphill. The ball will stop, and may even roll back, if you stop pushing. The upgrade is long, so don't use all your energy at the bottom. A steady flow of problems will come your way. The more problems you have anticipated, the more ready you will be to deal with them. In this way, they may not become crises. For example, in the program mentioned earlier (Russo, 1974) in which delinquents worked in a mental hospital, it was predicted that contraband would be brought into the delinquents' treatment center from the hospital and that sexual contacts would occur between the delinquent boys and the female patients and staff at the hospital. Tentative means of dealing with these kinds of problems were worked out in advance, and when such incidents occurred, they were handled with little fuss. The best protection against crises is preplanning, followed by open communication between the staff and administration. Your organization's policies and traditions may dictate the form of this communication; but, whatever the form, it should be frequent and open. It is especially important to give those who are against the change every chance to explain their point of view. If they are given a chance to disagree and be heard, they may change their minds.

Let's review some of the conditions that may help to make your attempt at change successful. Those who control resources, rewards, punishments, and contacts are more likely to effect change than those who lack such power. Can you identify these characteristics in the examples given in the past few pages? What were the resources—money, ideas, or something else? What were the rewards and punishments, and for whom were they intended? Who were the contacts? Did these examples contain all the characteristics needed for successful change?

If your clients are concerned, they may be of some help in keeping the change process going. Remember to respect the delicate position of the clients. Used carefully, pressure from clients can be effective. The use of client demands to help bring about a change needs to be included in the detailed planning and the detailed follow-up. To repeat an earlier caution, your clients may mean well, but they probably won't know quite what they are doing or why they are doing it. They will need leadership.

Conflict, Competition, and Cooperation

As noted earlier, most of us view conflict as a negative; however, conflict also can be viewed as a catalyst for change and the engine that keeps it moving.

Survival requires change. Organizational norms of apathy and "harmony at all costs" allow poor decisions to go unquestioned. Robbins (1974:9) claims that "more organizations are dying from complacency and apathy than are dying from an overabundance of conflict." The value of conflict in group decision making was clearly demonstrated by Kahn and Boulding (1964:147) when, as an experiment, they purposely placed deviants in some groups who were told to solve a problem. Other groups did not have a person who challenged and questioned the popular, or majority, position. In every case, the groups in which the deviants were placed came up with richer and more elegant solutions. But watch out! When each group was asked to oust one member, every group that contained a deviant member chose to drop that member.

Here, and in earlier chapters, I have come across as being in favor of conflict; however, I do not advocate all kinds and intensities of conflict. Some conflict is functional; it supports goals and improves performance. On the other hand, conflict can also be dysfunctional. The distinction between these two types of conflict isn't always clear. Those who value the status quo will view conflict differently than those who want change.

Compared to "conflict," the word "competition" is much more American. The free enterprise system is intended to be guided by competition. Competition for scarce resources can lead to conflict. In this kind of a situation, one party in the competition gains at the expense of the other, resulting in conflict. On the other hand, competition between departments, wards, cell blocks, or classes for the highest percentage of blood donors will not likely cause conflict. The point is that, although competition and conflict are two distinct concepts, they are sometimes related.

Many managers and supervisors believe that cooperation is the opposite of conflict. These people believe that, if they can stifle conflict, cooperation will result. This isn't so, especially in large bureaucratic organizations. Large formal structures produce both isolation and segregation. The organizational rewards available to key staff members come from the part of the organization for which you work, not the department with whom you cooperate. You and your clients will find some people who cooperate for reasons that have little to do with organizational reward. Use that cooperation with the knowledge that no one is being paid for it.

Remember, You're a Guest

If you are an intern, student teacher, or trainee, you shouldn't try to make any real changes in the organization in which you are receiving your training. You are there to see what the place is really like, not to change it. The host organization and your school have carefully agreed to the terms of your apprenticeship. If you violate those terms, your actions could cost future students the opportunity to have a work experience. If the experience is more false than real, tell your department chairperson or the dean; do not try to change the host organization while you are a student.

Clinical experiences for student teachers and nurses in college-degree programs are usually arranged in local schools and hospitals. Students' time and allegiance are shared by the teachers and the hospital supervisors. The student is subjected to the sometimes contradictory pronouncements and justifications of each group. The students can't remain neutral, because, while they're in school, the teaching faculty controls their destiny and their loyalty. Since the clinical experiences are brief in every specialty area, the student nurse does not have the time or the interest to develop loyalties to the hospital; however, after graduation, the conflict begins.

As a part of the university program, student teachers must perform for a university supervisor. And, as a part of the host school, they must perform to meet the standards of the cooperating teacher. Obviously, then, much of the value of student teaching is determined by the luck of the draw — the people to whom the student teachers are assigned by the university and the host school. The idea is to satisfy both the university supervisor and the cooperating teacher. The student teachers' position is usually compounded by a number of other things. For instance, student teachers are frequently placed in communities in which they have few friends. Moreover, they find it difficult to find apartments that are within a student's budget. At the host school, student teachers are treated with an abrupt kindness. Having been introduced to a few teachers, isolated student teachers seek them out during lunch periods and free hours. While other teachers are busy grading papers or talking about students they have had, student teachers feign interest or pretend to be engrossed in books. As a result, many student teachers feel comfortable only in the company of cooperating teachers and a few other colleagues, usually in the same age bracket. In fact, student teachers in secondary schools report that the students usually make them feel more comfortable than the faculty members do.

Your administrative superiors are neither idiots nor geniuses. They are people who feel good when they are respected, needed, and genuinely complimented. They feel bad when they are sick, threatened, and put down. When they are approached for advice and counsel or with well-conceived and carefully planned suggestions, many administrators will listen carefully, ask clarifying questions, and be generally supportive of staff members who want to improve services. It is a pleasure to have such an administrative superior.

When you try to make changes, remember that every organization is unique to some degree. Each organization has its own unique history, goals, and position in the larger social structure. Despite this fact, some responses to change are common to all organizations. For example, as Gamsen (1968:146) has pointed out, "When an organization has exhausted its supply of social controls, either because it has few available or because the attempted social controls were ineffective, organizational modification should occur."

Summary

At some point, your job as a human-service worker may seem like part of a sham. You are confronted by one agency, under bureaucrats, with liberty and service for some. You don't deal with real problems. You're busy applying bandages instead of antidotes — treating symptoms, not causes. You may want to make changes. First, you need to accept things as they are. Accepting doesn't mean becoming resigned to the status quo.

A number of examples in this chapter illustrate some of the conditions that may make your change efforts successful. Conflict, competition, and cooperation are important elements in the dynamics of change and survival. More important is the way in which you deal with the tension and anxiety that results from frustration.

Discussion Questions

1. In addition to talking to a friend and reading your personal journal, list some socially acceptable means of reducing job tension.

2. What would be the costs to you for going to the director (or dean) to try to make a change in the way things are done by your supervisor (or teacher)? What effect would your behavior have on your continuing relationship with your supervisor (or teacher)?

3. What is the relationship between your change (or proposed change) and the rest of the system? How are they linked? Can you change one part of a system without affecting the entire system?

4. What power do you have as a staff person or student?

References

Baer, B. L., and Federico, R. 1978. *Educating the Baccalaureate Social Worker.* Cambridge, MA: Ballinger Publishing Company.

Baldridge, J. V., and Burnham, R. A. 1975. Organizational innovation: Individual, organizational and environmental impacts. *Administrative Science Quarterly*, Summer, 20.

Buckley, W.F., Jr. 1986. Crucial steps in combatting the AIDS epidemic: Identify all the carriers. *New York Times*, March 18, p. A27.

Devito, R. A. 1974. The supervisory bypass: A symptom of organizational anxiety. *Hospital and Community Psychiatry*, 25(11).

Edelwich, J., and Brodsky, A. 1980. *Burn Out.* New York: Human Sciences Press.

French, W. L., and Bell, C. H., Jr. 1990. *Organization Development* (4th ed). Englewood Cliffs, NJ: Prentice-Hall.

Gamsen, Z. F. 1968. Organizational responses to members. *The Sociological Quarterly*, Spring.

Golden, O. 1990. Innovation in public sector human service programs: The implications of innovation by "groping along." *Journal of Policy Analysis and Management*, 9(2), 219-48.

Kahn, R. L., and Boulding, E. 1964. *Power and Conflict in Organizations.* New York: Basic Books.

Levy, L., and Herzog, A. N. 1971. The birth and demise of a planning unit in a state mental health department. *Community Mental Health*, September, 7(3).

Lynton, R. P. 1969. Linking an innovation subsystem into the system. *Administrative Science Quarterly*, September, 14(3).

Mandell, B. R., and Schram, B. 1985. *Human Services.* New York: John Wiley and Sons.

Maslach, C. 1986. *Burnout, The Cost of Caring.* Englewood Cliffs, NJ: Prentice-Hall.

Melaville, A. I., and Blank, M. R. 1991. What it takes: Structuring interagency partnerships to connect children and families with comprehensive services. *Education and Human Services Consortium.* Washington, D. C. January.

Robbins, S. P. 1974. *Managing Organizational Conflict: A New Traditional Approach.* Englewood Cliffs, NJ: Prentice-Hall.

Russo, J. R. 1974. Mutually Therapeutic Interaction Between Mental Patients and Delinquents. *Hospital and Community Psychiatry,* August, 25(8).

Schorr, E. B., and Schorr, D. 1989. *Within Our Reach.* New York: Doubleday.

Wade, L. L. 1967. Professionals in Organizations: A Neoteric Model. *Human Organization,* Spring and Summer, 26(1,2).

8 Prevention

An important human-service goal is to make clients' lives healthier and happier. The best way to do this is to keep any problems from occurring. While this can never be accomplished completely, much can be done through *prevention*. There has been significant growth in the number and types of prevention programs in the human-service field in the past decade. Along with the growth has come some confusion and uncertainty about what a prevention program is and what constitutes effective programming.

As will be seen later in this chapter, prevention is defined in many ways at many levels. Regardless of the definition, the term "prevention" implies that some negative event will occur unless something is done. That "something to be done" defines the program theory and many of the activities in which you will engage as a human-service worker. Said differently, problems will be created unless some form of intervention takes place to reduce the cause of the problem.

All prevention programs operate on some theory. These theories of causation are seldom explicit. Each of us has a set of beliefs about what causes problems in our society. Programs designed to prevent those problems are aimed at the cause. What are the factors you believe cause the problems?

1. *Educational issues*—poor achievement, inadequate teachers, no home support, poor educational materials, inappropriate instructional processes.

141

2. *Social issues*—lack of legitimate opportunities.

3. *Cultural issues*—ethnic prejudices and discrimination, historically poor self-esteem.

4. *Political issues*—democratic form of government.

5. *Medical issues*—poor diet, bad genetics, inadequate medical care.

6. *Economic issues*—capitalism, minimum wage, welfare system.

The organization for which you work has some program theory. Usually this theory is described at least implicitly in a *mission statement* of some sort. This mission statement may be focused on illicit drug use, law and order, education, physical health, economic situations, prejudice, self-esteem, legitimate employment opportunities, and so on. Exploring the program theory held by your employer may clarify the reasons for the programs your organization operates. More than likely you will be able to define your employer's program theory by adding up all of the programs your organization sponsors. That summation will point you in the direction of identifying the theory or theories under which your organization operates.

What is the national government's program theory regarding justice, health, education, and welfare? The answer appears to lie in two interrelated motives: (1) to avoid social unrest, and (2) to acquire or maintain political power.

Some would argue that the poor laws of England were enacted to reduce the activity of roving bands of beggars that often engaged in robbery or pillage. Similarly, the Civilian Conservation Corps that operated after the Great Depression was in response to the World War I veterans known as "bonus marchers" who, in 1932, were dispersed by a force of federal troops and housed in abandoned army camps. Similarly, in the late 1960s, the Job Corps Program housed urban youth in abandoned military camps. These governmental activities all could be viewed as an attempt to avoid social unrest.

Programs in health, education, and welfare designed to acquire or maintain political power are evident by the level of energy expended by competing political parties as they seek to take credit for some programs or avoid the blame for reductions in others. Even at the lowest level of government, often township or precinct, the general assistance program can be used for political purposes.

So what is your organization attempting to prevent? Crime, crack babies, adolescent pregnancy, ignorance, ethnic prejudice, disruption of foster care? At what level of prevention are you or do you plan to work? Some professionals work to minimize the number of deaths and injuries from gang wars. Others work to keep society safe from the criminally insane. Others provide hospice care to prevent inhumane death. Yet others work in organizations to prevent inhumane treatment for the severely mentally handicapped.

Discussions about prevention can cause conflict. Daily we are exposed to the debates surrounding issues such as birth control and abortion. The preeminence of these issues is highlighted in a report by the National Commission on Children (1991). The 400-page document was a consensus of 34 members except for the chapter on health. Nine members of that commission insisted on a minority chapter dealing with abstinence as the means of reducing the spread of AIDS and for preventing teenage pregnancy.

As a staff member, you may be caught up in this debate. Those who work in publicly funded organizations will have a constantly changing set of rules and regulations dealing with abortion and birth control. State legislatures and federal governments change their positions. Those who are employed by private agencies may be given direction reflecting the beliefs and the values of that agency.

Regardless of these rules and regulations about abortion and birth control, it is clear that many powerful antecedents of premature sexual activity and premature pregnancy have done their damage long before a youngster reaches childbearing age. Many of the strongest determinants of high rates of teenage childbearing originate far from where the vulnerable teenagers hang out, far from where they may drift into sexual relations, and far from where they may decide to use contraceptives. Prevention, if it is to be effective, is needed at several levels.

Experts may continue to debate the contribution of economic, psychological, and other earlier experiences, but we already know more than enough to act. As human-service workers, we must insure that disadvantaged young people acquire the needed skills and work habits to become connected to the world of work and achievement and have the opportunities to use their skills to earn a decent income. We must insure that young people believe and are convinced that they have a real stake in their own future. "Only then are they likely to believe in the value of postponing sex and childbearing" (Schorr and Schorr, 1989: 62).

More simply, prevention can be defined as efforts to reduce the incidence of problem behavior, undesirable events, or disorder. Incidence refers to the number of times a particular problem, event, or disorder occurs during a specified period (Mueller and Higgins, 1988). Prevention is an *active* rather than a *reactive* process. Prevention efforts are intended to keep something from happening and must, of necessity, occur before the fact. Prevention efforts are commonly categorized into primary, secondary, and tertiary.

Primary prevention activities are those which occur at lower levels of the system. These activities are typically more focused on those issues which are viewed as closer to being the cause of the problems. Parent effectiveness training, drug abuse prevention education, programs for at-risk children below school age, detoxification of drug abusing pregnant women, intensive family preservation services, nutrition programs, genetic counseling, and the like are examples of what are usually considered primary prevention activities.

The *secondary* level of prevention is what we commonly think of as treatment. Included are such programs as secure detention, mental health centers, remedial instruction, foster care, Headstart programs, homeless shelters, and probation. These programs are designed to reduce the effect or duration of a problem.

Tertiary prevention generally refers to either rehabilitation, or reducing the negative effects of a disability, discomfort, or of an existing disorder. For example, you may work in a hospice environment designed to prevent the inhumane treatment of the terminally ill.

Competent human-service workers are required at each of these levels of prevention. Personal satisfaction and professional reward is possible at any of these levels. To provide a humane and moderately educational environment for mentally retarded adults can be a most satisfying professional activity. Working in an urban police department facing violence and depravation on a daily basis, the recruit officer may have the opportunity to influence a small number of youth in positive ways. The value of this influence to both the recruit officer and to the youth may temporarily outweigh the effects of the degradation and violence.

Kinds of Prevention Programs

Prevention efforts are incorporated into a variety of services and programs. A close look at individual programs will help you identify the overall program theory and level of prevention where you are serving.

Infants

Programs to encourage regular prenatal care are becoming more available in some lower income areas. These areas have a much higher infant mortality rate than more affluent neighborhoods, as well as a greater incidence of low birth weight and prematurity. Infants who get a healthy start have a greater chance of avoiding numerous problems later on. Experts estimate that for every one dollar spent on prenatal care, three dollars is saved on medical care during the first year of the infant's life. Proper nutrition is another important factor in promoting healthy infants. The federal WIC program (Women, Infants, and Children) began in the 1970s to provide basic nutritional foods to needy families. Due to limited funding, only 59 percent of those eligible receive the benefits (Gibbs, 1990).

Prevention programs directed at improving the lives of high-risk infants require a wide variety of professional people. In addition to the medical personnel, such cases require home visitors, case managers, program evaluators, and counselors. Five programs of this type are described in *Fourteen Ounces of Prevention* (Price et al., 1988). "All of the programs have been effective with high-risk populations whose access to educational, economic, health, and other salient resources is seriously limited." All five . . . "share at their core a common ecological understanding of behavior, which is reflected in efforts to enhance child development by strengthening parents and relevant systems as well as individual children. They also share cultural sensitivity and attention to the details that operationalize the interventions" (p. 8). These can be rewarding programs in which to work.

Early age intervention is essential to the survival of our culture.

- "At least one-third of the nation's children are at risk of school failure even before they enter kindergarten.

- Since 1987, one-fourth of all preschool children in the United States have been in poverty.

- Every year, about 350,000 children are born to mothers who were addicted to cocaine during pregnancy.

- Twenty percent of America's preschool children have not been vaccinated against polio.

- The "Norman Rockwell" family—a working father, a housewife mother, and two children of school age—constitutes only six percent of U.S. households today.

- One-fourth of pregnant mothers receive no physical care of any sort during the crucial first trimester of pregnancy.

- At least two million school-age children have no adult supervision at all after school. Two million more are being reared by neither parent.
- On any given night, between 50,000 and 200,000 children have no home. (In 1988, forty percent of shelter users were families with children.)
- About one-third of preschool children are destined for school failure because of poverty, neglect, sickness, handicapping conditions, and lack of adult protection and nurturance" (Hodgkinson, 1991:9).

Children in School

Despite the many organizational obstacles that confront teachers and others who work in schools, educational institutions still represent one of the best environments for successful prevention activities.

Infants and children are flexible and adaptable to their environment, and are therefore ideal recipients of prevention intervention. A logical setting to provide such programs for children is in the school (Alpert, 1985; Price et al., 1988). The thirty or more hours per week that children spend at school can be used to develop the whole child, not just the educational aspect. Teachers and other human-service workers can be trained to be aware of risk factors and signs of abuse or maladjustment. They can implement effective programs that can easily reach the individuals in need. Often with extra effort they can involve the parents.

School-based programs to deal with such problems as delinquency, drug abuse, and teen pregnancies are sometimes necessary and possible. One teacher (Kramer, 1988) has developed an elective course to deal with what she considers the root causes of many students' problems. These causes are: (1) lack of self-esteem and self-respect, (2) inability to communicate thoughts and feelings on an intimate and genuine level, (3) few, if any, conflict resolution or decision-making skills, (4) unrealistic expectations about how life was supposed to be, and (5) a complete misunderstanding between men and women who, as a result of quite different upbringings, have different ideas about how to approach life and how to live it.

The elective course attempts to develop in students:

- "a strong and secure sense of self-worth to help them say no to drugs, alcohol, irresponsible sex, and other harmful or self-destructive behaviors;
- communication skills to help them interact better with others and handle anger and conflict safely;

- ability to cope with disappointment, rejection, and loss;
- the understanding that violence is never acceptable and that it never solves problems, it simply makes them worse;
- clear and realistic expectations about their roles in all relationships — friendships, love, marriage, parenting, and the career world" (p. 57).

Selected teachers were given intensive training in the use of various strategies to accomplish these objectives. Role playing, group discussions, readings, peer facilitating, guest speakers, and other techniques were utilized. The teachers reported positive results and a dramatic impact on students' self-esteem.

The elective course has focused on adolescents with positive results. The course may be even more effective when adapted and offered to younger children. Teen pregnancies, suicide, substance abuse, and delinquency could be reduced considerably, thereby affecting "the lives not only of the direct recipients of preventive services but also of other members of their families, their peers, and significant others in their environments" (Rochefort, 1989:4269). Especially in terms of tight budgets, such classes may have to compete with the three R's for survival. Teachers and other school employees might wish to explore this type of curriculum content further.

A nationwide series of conferences was held to develop models for preventing teenage alcohol and other drug problems. The results were published in *Prevention Plus: Involving Schools, Parents, and the Community in Alcohol and Drug Education* (1984) referenced at the end of this chapter. Five programs are described in detail and innovative ideas are also presented. Examples of the vast diversity in preventive approaches that are being implemented in the school system are included.

Lifelong Prevention

Prevention is not just for children. Many life transitions occur during adulthood, and many of the problems associated with them can be reduced or avoided with proper timing and appropriate programs (Price et al., 1988; Rochefort, 1989). These transitions include positive changes such as marriage and the birth of a child as well as the obviously traumatic events, i.e., death of a spouse or divorce. All such transitions require major adjustment that can lead to stress and other disorders. A wide variety of professional staff roles exist in programs that focus on adult clients. Some younger professionals may overlook such jobs because they lack the wisdom of age and feel they would not be accepted by adults. Yet youthful professionals working with adults is certainly no less valid than celibate priests doing premarital counseling.

Other professional roles exist in religious and secular organizations offering classes for couples planning to marry. These classes often attempt to confront issues that couples may overlook or feel uncomfortable discussing — such as money management, number of children desired and childrearing beliefs, sexuality, and gender role expectations. While little empirical data is available, these classes have potential benefits and may make the adjustment easier.

Hospitals, Lamaze, and other groups teach childbirth preparation to expectant parents. Prepared couples tend to require less medication and are able to assist in the birthing process more. This results in a more enjoyable event and a healthier baby, and may improve the parent/child bonding. Additional classes are often available in infant care, nutrition, and related issues. These provide the potential for a healthier environment for both infants and parents.

There are a variety of support and therapy groups available for people dealing with divorce or widowhood. A program implemented by Silverman called "Widow-to-Widow" has shown positive results. "Widows contact newly bereaved women to offer one-on-one support. Telephone calls, home visits, and small group meetings are used to provide social support and mutual help. Research on Widow-to-Widow programs indicates that participants show improved mood, lower anxiety, and better social integration and progress more rapidly in the course of adaptation than do widows who do not participate in the program" (Price et al., 1988:140).

The aged can also benefit from programs that offer medical and housekeeping assistance, home-delivered meals, and transportation to social, medical, and recreational activities. Providing these types of aid encourages a more independent lifestyle by making it possible for many of the elderly to remain in their homes. Better health and psychological well-being are promoted, as well as the obvious financial benefits in reducing medical costs and nursing home or hospital placement. Both private and public organizations sponsor programs to prevent out-of-home placements for the elderly. These programs require employees who can appreciate that every single day an elderly person was happy at home makes their job worthwhile.

Medical Prevention

Medical prevention has been practiced for many years and is one of the most widely recognized prevention efforts. There are immunizations available for a variety of illnesses, including diphtheria, poliomyelitis, smallpox, rubella, influenza, and measles. "For children the most basic requirement is inoculation, the surest way to spare a child—and the health-care system—the ravages of tuberculosis, polio, measles, and whooping cough. During the first twenty years after the discovery of the measles vaccine, public-health experts estimate more than five billion dollars was saved in medical costs, not to mention countless lives" (Gibbs, 1990:42).

There have been environmental changes accomplished in the twentieth century that can be attributed to primary medical prevention. These include improvements in water and milk supplies and sewage disposal systems (Felner et al., 1983). The iodizing of salt has all but eliminated certain thyroid conditions and cretinism, which leads to severe mental retardation. Lead paint regulations and pollution controls (although these may not be sufficient) are additional ways to strive to maintain good health. There has been a growing awareness that similar efforts can be made to prevent psychological and social problems. In many cases these problems result from the same factors as medical conditions, e.g., inadequate prenatal care or poor nutrition. "A national survey in 1988 found that two-thirds of teachers reported poor health among children to be a 'learning problem'. This is why Headstart, the model federal program providing quality preschool for poor children, also includes annual medical and dental screenings" (Gibbs, 1990:43).

Prevention interventions are most effective when they are directed to the individuals most in need, the people at risk for specific problems. Does your job deal with predisposing factors that occur before the appearance of problem symptoms, e.g., gender, age, family history, social class, education, occupation, or income? Or does your responsibility include the prevention of precipitating factors? Life strain, daily stress, and major life transitions (Rochefort, 1989) often occur just before the onset of symptoms and may trigger the onset of problems.

Components of Effective Prevention Programs

Many highly praised and widely publicized prevention programs have not proven to be effective. An excellent source of such "programs that don't work" is the work of Wells and Biegel (1991) referenced at the end of the chapter. A less expensive book for your professional library is *The Technology of Prevention Workbook* (Lofquist, 1989).

A number of key program components or significant factors associated with prevention programs that *do* work have been identified (Mueller and Higgins, 1988). These factors or program components are based on empirical evidence drawn from effectiveness studies in four broad program areas: (1) Child abuse and neglect, (2) poor school performance and school failure, (3) teenage pregnancy, and (4) teenage substance abuse. While these components are not intended to be an all-inclusive list, they do provide some insights into effective prevention programming.

1. *The capacity to identify a population at risk for the problem to be prevented.* Although current knowledge of risk factors is far from perfect, certain populations have been identified as being at significant risk for developing problems. For example: poverty, poor relationships with parents, and nonconformity have been associated with teenage substance abuse, school failure, and the like. At-risk populations are generally defined by the presence of multiple characteristics rather than a single one. The ability to identify such a target population is crucial to the development of an effective prevention effort.

2. *The ability to reach an at-risk population with the program.* If a prevention program is to be effective (reduces the incidence of a given problem), it must not only be able to identify persons at risk for developing the problem, but it must be able to reach them with its intervention as well. Several studies have indicated that those people who are at highest risk for a problem benefit most from prevention programs.

3. *The appropriateness of the timing of the prevention intervention.* The timing of prevention interventions relative to human development or life experiences is crucial to their success or failure. For example, the timing of programs to prevent teenage pregnancies must occur before substantial numbers of young girls become sexually active.

4. *The duration and intensity of the program.* Generally speaking, prevention programs do not lend themselves to brief intervention or overnight solutions. With a few exceptions, most interventions are more effective when they are of longer duration and are of greater intensity. For many prevention programs, periodic "booster" sessions to reinforce new skills and knowledge add to program effectiveness.

5. *The ability to address several risk factors.* In most situations, those programs that are able to address more risk factors for

a problem are more likely to be successful than those that address only one.

6. *Experiential learning techniques in educational programs.* Prevention programs that are essentially educational interventions are most effective if they use experiential learning techniques. Programs that require only passive listening of the participants (e.g., films, videos, lectures), are unlikely to be as potent in changing behavior.

7. *Parental involvement in programs focusing on children and adolescents.* Parental involvement is a desirable feature of many prevention programs aimed at children and adolescents. Such involvement permits risk factors for the problem to be addressed not only at the individual-child level but also at the family level. This in turn strengthens the potential effectiveness of the program.

8. *Highly skilled, well-trained, prevention program staff.* Effective prevention programs tend to have well-trained, often highly skilled staff. If paraprofessionals are used in prevention programs, it is critical that they be well-trained and under professional supervision. Prevention programs dealing with children are most effective when there is a high staff-to-child ratio.

9. *Program structure and integration/collaboration with other community services.* A high level of structure, particularly in programs for children, has been related to program effectiveness. Structure for this type of program includes clearly defined instructional objectives tied to overall program objectives, planning of program activities, training of staff in the methods and content of the program, and strong leadership and supervision of staff. Cooperation and coordination among community organizations are also seen as important to program effectiveness.

10. *Simplicity of prevention messages.* Those prevention programs that have simple, clear goals tend to be more effective than those that have more complex or less clearly defined outcome goals.

11. *Sensitivity to potential adverse effects.* If a prevention program is not benign in its effect but has some potency, there is at least the potential for adverse or unforeseen negative consequences. One unintended negative consequence may be arousing unnecessary fears in children who have participated in sexual abuse prevention programs. Another negative consequence which should be avoided is the "labeling" of program

participants. Because of limited resources, prevention programs often restrict eligibility to those at very high risk for a particular problem. This may result in an image problem for the program, and may inadvertently stigmatize those who participate. Sensitivity to potential adverse effects such as these is necessary for effective prevention programming.

Research conducted by the American Psychological Association Task Force on Promotion, Prevention, and Intervention Alternatives confirmed these eleven successful program components, and added to them the rigorous evaluation of prevention programs (Price et al., 1989). Efforts to document, describe, and analyze what takes place in a prevention program can help give the program direction and keep it on course. If the results of a prevention program are positive, it can encourage decision makers to persist in prevention efforts. Documented success also can help to establish the validity of the methods utilized. Less welcome by administrators, funders, and dedicated employees are program evaluations that are less than expected (Wells and Biegel, 1991). However, if a prevention program evaluation indicates that the program is not succeeding or is having negative, unintended results, there is basis for discontinuing or redirecting the prevention effort.

Summary

The benefits of prevention are clear, both in quality of life and in cost. Unfortunately the specific results are sometimes difficult to measure and may take many years to show true impact. "To be really good, prevention should be unnoticed, because one never knows which individuals in a population at risk would have gotten sick had there been no prevention" (Felner et al., 1983: 310). The money saved is difficult to calculate because health and social problems have so many possible considerations in addition to the actual disorder. Implementation of many more programs and systematic evaluation with an organized dissemination of effective interventions need to be accomplished before public and professional support will be given fully (Felner et al., 1983; Gibbs, 1990; Pepper, 1987; Price et al., 1988; Rochefort, 1989). Only then will the funds be made available, and only then will the effects begin to make a real impact.

Those of you who work in a job that is focused on prevention will need to have a clear program theory and the skill to communicate to your public. Successful outcomes of your prevention efforts may be invisible. "If primary prevention is done really well, nobody much knows that it was done at all" (Felner et al., 1983: 310).

Discussion Questions

1. Taking a broad view, list the prevention activities that enabled you to become a college student and/or a successful professional.
2. In what stage(s) of your development were these prevention activities most effective?
3. Think about one of your high school peers that "didn't make it." For him or her to have made it, what prevention activities would have been required and at what stages in his or her development?

References

Alpert, J. L. 1985. Change within a profession: Change, future, prevention, and school psychology. *American Psychologist*, October, 1112-21.

Felner, R. D., Jason, L. A., Moritsugu, J. N., and Farber, S. S. 1983. *Preventive Psychology*. New York: Pergamon Press.

Gibbs, N. 1990. Shameful bequests to the next generation. *Time*, October 8.

Hodgkinson, H. 1991. Reform versus reality. *Phi Delta Kappan*, September, 73, 8-16.

Kramer, P. 1988. A preventive approach to adolescent problems. *Educational Leadership*, March, 56-57.

Lofquist, W. A. 1989. *The Technology of Prevention Handbook*. Tucson, AZ: AYD Publications.

Mueller, D. P., and Higgins, P. S. 1988. *Funders Guide Manual: A Guide to Prevention Programs in Human Services*. St. Paul, MN: Amherst H. Wilder Foundation.

National Commission on Children. 1991. *Beyond Rhetoric: A New American Agenda for Children and Families*. Washington, DC: U.S. Government Printing Office.

National Institute on Alcohol Abuse and Alcoholism. 1984. *Prevention Plus: Involving Schools, Parents, and the Community in Alcohol and Drug Education*. Rockville, MD: United States Department of Health and Human Services.

Pepper, B. 1987. A public policy for the long-term mentally ill: A positive alternative to reinstitutionalization. *American Journal of Orthopsychiatry*, July, 57 (3):452-57.

Price, R. H., Cowen, E. L., Lorion, R. P., and Ramos-McKay, J. 1988. *Fourteen Ounces of Prevention*. Washington, DC: American Psychological Association.

Price, R. H., Cowen, E. L., Lorion, R. P., and Ramos-McKay, J. 1989. The search for effective prevention programs: What we learned along the way. *American Journal of Orthopsychiatry*, January, 59 (1):49-58.

Rochefort, D. A. 1989. *Handbook on Mental Health Policy in the United States*. New York: Greenwood Press.

Schorr, L.B. and Schorr, D. 1989. *Within Our Reach*. New York: Doubleday.

Wells, K. and Biegel, D. E. (eds.) 1991. *Family Preservation Services*. Newbury Park, CA: Sage Publications, Inc.

9 Odds and Ends From the Present and a Look at the Future

In this chapter we will briefly touch on some of the operational aspects of human-service organizations, including committees, consultants, and accreditation, as well as current issues in the workplace, such as sexual harassment. We will also take a look at trends in human-service delivery and what they mean for the future, both for help givers and clients.

Human-Service Organizations

Committees

Like almost everything else in bureaucratic organizations, committees can be ranked in order of importance. Committees that deal with organizational structure have the highest bureaucratic status, and those that deal with client welfare have the lowest status; the others fall somewhere between these two. Promotion, salary, and hiring committees are near the top. Those dealing with routine organizational maintenance, such as revising of paper forms or planning the staff party, are near the bottom. Somewhere in the middle are task forces, which administrators call committees, if they think they might be important. For a more detailed and delightfully funny description of committee hierarchy, read Kolstoe's *College Professoring* (1975).

As a staff member, you will have an opportunity to be appointed or elected to various committees. If you are a good committee member, the chance for more service to the organization will follow quickly. If you are really good, you could become a committee chairperson. Good committee members attend, are attentive, speak a little, and volunteer to help write the committee report. Look at your organization's committee structure, how it operates, what it accomplishes, and where you want to participate—if at all.

Consultants

Almost all organizations use *consultants*—people who are brought in to advise on specific areas or problems. Usually, they're paid by the day—their pay is called an *honorarium*. Consultants are chosen because they are well-known in a particular field, have important contacts, believe what the boss believes, or, more often, because they used your boss as a consultant last year. For whatever reason they are chosen, and regardless of how much they are paid, you will see little of them and be only temporarily (if at all) influenced by them or their report. Prior to their arrival, you will be told to be honest in answering their questions. It is not unusual for a consultant to come in before your organization is due to be accredited, inspected, or evaluated. A good report from a consultant can be used to impress outside evaluators.

Accrediting, Inspecting, and Evaluating Human-Service Organizations

On a regular basis, your organization will be examined by a state, regional, or national body to see that it meets some minimum standards. You will know when one of these visits is about to occur. The organization's paperwork will be put in order. You will be asked to look over your own personnel file to see that all of your latest training, honors, publications, and other achievements have been listed. Hospital staffs will scramble to keep their nursing-care plans up to date. Shoddy-looking areas will be painted. In residential institutions, menus may change a bit and windows will be washed. Vacations may be arranged for certain people during the time the evaluation team is present. Before outside evaluators arrive, you will be told to behave openly and honestly with them. At times, these inspectors interview clients. It will be interesting for you to see how clients are chosen for this audience.

In-Service Training

There are three major types of in-service training programs. The traditional in-service day is found in all public schools. The day may consist of as many as five days sprinkled throughout the year. For those teachers who haven't made arrangements to play golf or work in their home gardens, the in-service sessions follow a format of introductions that precede a speech by the regional big boss. One teacher describes the first in-service day of the school term this way:

> The speech always starts out with an interesting and amusing story about little Johnny at school and is usually supplemented by something clever, like "Be a 'FAR' out teacher." The F stands for 'fair but firm,' the A for 'accountable,' and the R for 'relevant.'"
>
> After coffee break, which is usually extended for as long as possible, the superintendent of the school region makes his statement. The speech will, of course, evolve around the following words or phrases: "teachers are special people," "sacred obligation," "build better citizens," "concerned individuals," "guiding light of community," "each student is a precious gem, light, popcorn ball," etc., ad infinitum. The speech is concluded with "let's make this the best year of our educational career."

Mental-health agencies and social-welfare agencies have changed this traditional structure somewhat; they refer to in-service days as regional conferences. These conferences are held at large restaurants. Instead of textbook publishers' displays at the teacher workshops, new and innovative programs are described by a long series of speakers. The greatest benefit that staff members can derive from these conferences is a chance to see coworkers in a setting outside the agency. Perhaps more important is the opportunity to become acquainted with someone who may be a future referral resource for clients.

The second type of in-service training is run by outsiders — for example, an extension class taught by a professor from a local university, or an expert working with staff members on a specific problem. The value of this type of in-service training depends completely on the quality of the teachers and on the staff who are the students. Some organizations even allow and encourage staff members to take advantage of such training on company time.

The third type of in-service training takes place outside the organization. Many help-giving agencies are encouraging staff members to obtain additional education; in some cases, the agency pays the tuition. Read the fine print when you accept tuition money from your agency. How much do you have to repay if you quit before a certain period of time? An additional caution: education, like many other time-honored institutions, has been affected by the profit motive. There are literally hundreds of educational institutions operating as profit-making enterprises and using the lure of college credit for "life experiences" as a marketing strategy. Some of these institutions have exceptionally high standards; others are diploma mills. Be sure you know the difference before you spend time and money.

The professional conference is another form of outside education. You should attend at least one such conference. You will be amazed to see how people behave away from home. Alcohol becomes the focus of much activity. Hospitality rooms with alcohol will be sponsored by organizations such as textbook publishers, equipment manufacturers, and professional service providers. My suggestion would be to spend your time with a glass of carbonated water and lemon slice, thus making your observations with a clear head. These informal meetings in hospitality rooms can be used to expand both your professional and personal network.

Job-Related Sex

People who are searching for the answer to "Who am I?" use sexual activity to take the place of other achievements. Otherwise healthy and competent people may try to boost their egos through a series of sexual encounters. Moreover, many lonely adults try to use sex to take the place of love. If you become involved with either of these two types of people, perhaps you, as one of their partners, might benefit by taking a look at your own needs and motives.

Many people treat sex very casually. One-sixth of all married adults admit to having affairs (Krauthammer, 1992). In a school setting, one consequence of this behavior can be to damage kids' role models:

> I have a friend—a good friend—who's been married for four years. One of the coaches, the same one who approached me time and time again, approached her. Well, she was having problems. This was her first year teaching, and she was impressed with his flattery and enthusiasms. She had an affair with the man. The three of us were free during the same hour, and I sat back,

and I watched things: the girl running to get dressed up after a class, making sure that her makeup was fine and her hair combed. The affair is going on now. She has left her husband. What people do is fine, but in school you do set an example. The kids see this so much.

A parallel incident that occurred in one agency could have happened anywhere:

The secretary would always come in late [Thursday] and have to put on her makeup and everything once she got there. I guess Wednesday night is her night out with this guy. People had caught them in different rooms together and stuff like that. Once, there was a big fight over it, like right there when his wife came down—I mean really a wild type thing.

The list of negative consequences of job-related sex is long. Some questions that bear consideration are:

What happens when the affair ends?

What happens to the normal lines of authority?

Does it affect work output?

What is the effect on regular channels of communication and information flow?

Sexual Harassment

Up to this point, we have discussed mutually consenting partners. Sexual harassment may exist when one person endures verbal or physical sexual advances from a coworker or supervisor. Sexual harassment in the workplace is an age old phenomenon. Events such as the confirmation hearings of Supreme Court Justice Clarence Thomas have served to focus attention on sexual harassment.

Sexual harassment defies a simple definition and solution. It is a complex problem with psychological, interpersonal, and socio-cultural causes and consequences (Gutek, 1985). Many organizations have recognized that they have both a legal and moral obligation to protect clients and employees from sexual harassment. One response has been to develop policies and procedures to assist those who feel sexually harassed. As discussed in earlier chapters, organizational culture is essentially a set of key values, beliefs, and norms that are socially acquired and shared by members of the organization. It seems reasonable that the key to sexual harassment prevention lies within the organizational value system and social influence processes (Thomann, Strickland, and Gibbons, 1989).

The culture in many organizations has not made the prevention of sexual harassment a high priority. Such inaction is not uncommon even in light of longstanding federal legislation (the 1964 Civil Right Act, Title VII, and the Education Amendment Act of 1972). What do you do if you are subjected to sexual harassment? What if you see clients being sexually harassed or abused? Your socialization agent or coach (Chapter 2) may be one place to start. Former teachers can sometimes help. Perhaps your employer has a policy on sexual harassment. Maybe it was included in the material you were given during orientation. If you ask the boss for a copy of the policy, you may be unintentionally sounding an alert. If you have a trusted fellow employee, use him or her. One of the first problems usually encountered in such a situation is the definition of sexual harassment.

Even though it may not begin as harassment, casual sexual intimacy between staff members and clients is potentially dangerous. In residential custodial institutions, there is a special problem for staff members who don't have their heads together. It is not unusual for clients who feel confused and powerless to try seduction as a means of obtaining special treatment. To accept their sexual offers is not only unethical but damaging to the institution and to your occupational effectiveness and future career. One specific case will illustrate this point:

> A young female employee has been having sexual relations with a patient on the ward. It has become so obvious, because the employee comes in on her days off to visit the patient. I mean, everybody has started wondering about it. It's so obvious. Here is somebody balling a client. How can she refuse if the client wants to have illegal visitors on the ward or make illegal telephone calls? It's gotten to a situation that's really ridiculous. Now we have started getting dope on the ward, and they can't figure out how.

Bureaucratic Celebrations and Sympathy

Office Christmas parties, annual staff picnics, and parties at the boss's home can be fun and interesting. Meeting your coworkers' spouses, friends, and children can give you a new appreciation of the staff. However, these events are always a bit uncomfortable, especially for those who aren't members of the staff. You try to tell your significant other about everybody who will be there before you go, and they try to remember names and act polite, but neither of you really chooses to spend time with this group. It's an obligation that you have. Even if the event is for staff members only, they may not be people you would choose for recreation. These events are usually planned by an informal committee, headed by the same people year after year. Before you try to change any aspects of these functions, take a look at the relevant norms. Does everybody draw names at Christmas? Does every staff member give the boss a present?

In addition to your personal reaction, how does the organization express sympathy to a coworker during a time of sadness or sickness? Death and illness evoke feelings. Flowers are sometimes sent to express such feelings. In a large work group, not all members want to or are able to send a fifty-dollar floral arrangement to the funeral. Your organization most likely has developed a procedure whereby each staff member contributes a certain amount. Usually, someone in the organization accepts the job of arranging such giving, collecting, and ordering to get the expression of sympathy to the right place at the right time.

Changes in Staff Members

Your new job may be challenging and rewarding, but you may see some things that need to be changed. Other staff members are trying to change and grow in their own ways. All are trying to reduce the emotional noise with which they have to live. Each of us has a private world that we don't often share with others. By sharing the portion of your private world that is associated with your job, you may help your coworkers to share their private job-related thoughts with you. Like all other social exchanges, such sharing will be done selectively. Levels of trust will be tested. Two people can form the beginning of a psychological support system. The job-related support system can be enlarged to include staff members whose concerns are similar. Such an informal group may be used to test ideas and share frustrations. A glimpse into a portion of two changing private worlds might give you some clues as to what might be going on in the heads of some of your coworkers. One teacher had this to share:

> I've really reached the conclusion after just two years that I'm
> not going to change the system. It will be changed, and I will
> gladly be a part of that change whenever we clean house. But
> one thing I do care about is those kids, and if something's not
> working and they're just hating coming to that class, I try to
> change it. I survived, and, going to my third year, I can see where
> I'm going to have much more freedom. I'm going to say, "Hey,

look. This is the way I feel." And, as of right now, I really don't care if other teachers want to say, "What does she think she's doing? Trying to be assistant principal, or is she bucking for a new job, or does she want an increase in pay?" I feel that's their problem, not mine.

A man who had been a prison guard for eight years describes the change that he went through. If you had been working with him, it might have been difficult to believe what you saw. He describes it this way:

> From the time I started, I had been punitive oriented. I believed that you must restrain men, teach them a lesson, punish them for violation of rules and regulations, and keep constant and strict security regulations within the institution. However, I began to wonder about some of these things, and I wondered if they were really necessary to the degree that they were being used. About this same time, we had a change in wardens and a change in philosophy in the department. I started to attend _____ State University to answer some of the questions that I had about human behavior. Before, I would average close to four or five tickets a day. This has dropped off. I have found myself able to talk with inmates and get more done than by threatening them or writing a ticket. I found that, within six months, my name as a ticket writer had been dropped. I found that inmates were willing to come up and talk with me about their problems.

Feelings of Failure

When you plunge in full steam ahead with all dedication and no realism, you set yourself up to fail. Go slowly. When you're not sensitive to your own emotions and needs, it's impossible to see clients clearly. Even when you think you know what is happening, you will be taken in ways that you don't understand. You will feel used, conned, or hustled. Somewhere, you learned that it was wrong to let clients use you—to let them get by with something. When it happens (and it will), the event could lead to the unhappy ending of a relationship. You could see all that you've tried to do as a waste of time; however, there is another way to look at it. The event may be made therapeutic. A real-life example of this kind can be used as a place to really begin helping. It can become a critical incident. It can make your expectations regarding clients more realistic. By confronting clients, you can help them to be more honest with you.

No matter how much you care, show concern, or even love, students will quit, inmates will mess up, patients will die, depressives will commit suicide, and parolees will violate the conditions of their parole. It's natural to feel that a portion of the failure is your responsibility. Maybe you really did the best you could. If you had it to do over again, perhaps you would do some things differently. Perhaps that will help you with the next challenge. Failure is especially hard on the new staff member who is fired up with humanitarian zeal to help, to give, and to serve. Your own well-being and sanity may be at stake if you accept more than your portion of any failures. More often, after the situation cools off, you'll find out that little or none of the failure was yours.

Don't Lose Your Keys

As professional helpers, we enter clients' private worlds. We invade their privacy, sometimes to the extreme of stripping them of clothes, cutting their hair, examining their bodily openings, and assigning them numbers in place of their names. Psychoanalysis, therapy, counseling, interviewing, and record keeping may be commonplace to you, but not to the clients. Their privacy becomes public record to you and others. Our society, with its government agencies and computers, is challenging privacy. We all need to hang on to our own private worlds. We need privacy, and we try to protect it. At times, the protection is more symbolic than real, more fragile than strong.

Drawn curtains, glass windows, and four-foot-high office dividers provide little real protection of our privacy; they are symbolic dividing lines between what is us and ours and what is others' and public. At the other extreme are elaborate electronic security systems. The most common means of protecting privacy is a lock, but locks also can be used to take away privacy. It is not the lock that provides privacy; it is the key to the lock (Manning, 1972).

The importance of locks and keys ranges from privacy in the family bathroom to arming a thermonuclear weapon. Bureaucratic organizations value locks and keys. They follow complicated procedures in distributing keys, keeping track of who has what keys, and punishing those who lose their keys. You will be able to determine who has the most status in your organization, because his or her key will open the most locks — this person may even have a master key. There are at least two exceptions to this rule: (1) the janitor may have a master key, and (2) the boss may not carry a key. Most likely, your keys open doors only in those areas of the institution that are relevant to your job.

What happens when you lose your keys? I lost the keys that were issued to me by the university and was interviewed by a security officer. "Where did you lose them?" "Well, if I knew, I would find them." "When did you lose them?" "I'm not really sure. Sometime between when I had them and now." "Did you look for them? Who helped you look? Did you tell these people what the keys opened? Do they work for the university?" After about forty minutes, I was told that, within the next week, I could come back to the security office and pick up a duplicate set of keys, if my supervisor approved. I had to pay two dollars for each lost key.

If you lose a metallic key, the locks can be changed to maintain physical security. At times, we treat the keys to our mental health as though they were the two-dollar variety. It's only when we start to lose these mental-health keys that we realize their value. Help givers are poor help takers. Helping other people can be an exhausting job, both physically and mentally. Treat the keys to your mental health with care. If you misplace them, ask for help in your search. Although you might be able to find the lost keys without help, the longer you search privately, the harder it will be to remember what your keys looked like.

A Look at the Future

We are rushing into the future. Apparently, nothing can stop the technological rampage. During the 1970s the United States enacted a nationwide fifty-five-mile speed limit. That didn't last long. Currently, if all who violated the sixty-five-mile limit were arrested, traffic would all but halt on the interstate system. We are in a hurry. Each generation has its excuse for the headlong rush.

Domestic social problems of the future are rushing toward us at an even faster rate — they had a head start. Many large cities are the scenes of riots, internally rotten public schools, affluent new industries with tax breaks, and increasing populations of poor black, white, and Hispanic peoples. Official poverty rates continue to increase. In the early 1990s, it was estimated that nearly one-fourth of all children in the United States live below the poverty level (Gibbs, 1990:43). The recognition of the extent of child abuse — especially sexual abuse — has begun to emerge. Estimates as high as one in five female children and one in seven male children having been victims of sexual abuse are not uncommon. Public discussion of this phenomenon was legitimized by celebrities ranging from beauty queens to talk show hosts. More than 10 percent of newborns show evidence of being affected by the mother's substance abuse (Weston et al., 1989). This explosion in the number of drug-exposed babies and drug-using parents threatens to overwhelm the already overtaxed foster care system. These medically fragile infants entering foster care creates a new set of demands on foster families and the human-service workers whose job it is to support these families. Hospital employees will see more boarder babies — infants remaining in hospitals because of an insufficient supply of foster homes adequate to meet their extensive medical needs (White et al., 1990).

Removing these newborn infants from the mothers' custody even before they go home will be a practice that is challenged more frequently. Such families are being destroyed after having struggled against the odds created by poverty and living on the margin where drug use is an integral part of the culture. Those who work with drug-exposed infants, their families, or their foster families will face issues that are as intellectually, emotionally, and ethically difficult as any that confront human-service workers.

Although often publicized as being related to poverty, such social problems as incest, child abuse, and drug abuse are not limited to the low socio-economic classes. Those with medical insurance do not represent an obvious drain on the economy (except for the higher premiums that all of us must pay). People considered "social problems" are those who do not have insurance. One response to this crushing demand on publicly funded social and medical service systems is to do more in prevention. Such efforts range from the "Just Say No" program to very serious attempts at family preservation activities.

National support for programs to protect children and prevent such problems will become more popular as legislators shift their focus toward prevention. The early 1990s saw the emergence of a variety of "Family Preservation Programs." One of the major challenges for the human-service worker of the future will be to have the skills and abilities to demonstrate that such prevention programs are an effective and efficient way to deal with the flood of demands which confront the current treatment system.*

Drug Abuse Treatment

In many parts of the United States, there was an excess of hospital beds in the 1980s which resulted in the bankruptcy and closure of many smaller and some larger hospitals in both urban and rural

---

* See *Services Integration for Families and Children in Crisis*, Office of Inspector General (HHS), OEI 09-90-00890, January, 1991.

areas. Partly as a response to these poor economic times for hospitals, hospital-based substance abuse treatment programs became quite popular. The media, including television, was used for the recruitment of patients. Those with insurance were welcomed into residential treatment centers. Typically insurance companies supported patients for about thirty days in chemical dependency treatment.

More than half of the patients who enter such programs have been through treatment multiple times (Fingarette, 1988). Insurance companies are beginning to realize that patients are receiving the same treatment, the same information, and the same program each time they are admitted. It would appear that there is something going on besides chemical dependency. Perhaps the individual under treatment needs to try something different — possibly out-patient care. As more and more insurance companies become less supportive of multiple admissions for the same policyholder, the competition between such residential programs will increase. Bankruptcy rates for drug abuse treatment facilities will increase.

The issue of alcoholism as a disease is not settled. Those with the "disease" viewpoint won a major victory when they successfully got the medical/psychiatric community to include alcoholism in a widely accepted diagnostic manual for discussion. It is interesting to note that most diseases are defined by physical symptoms and usually treated with medication. Alcoholism and many other substance abuse disorders are treated medically during a detoxification period lasting usually less than one week. For the remainder of the treatment, most programs use knowledge and spirituality — not medication.

Currently, there isn't any medication that prevents a person from becoming drug dependent. *Antabuse* is a drug which causes rather violent physical reactions when the person using it consumes alcohol. Antabuse is used as a part of an aversion therapy model in the rarest of cases. Many people would claim that substance abuse, including alcoholism, is a behavior — not a disease (Peele, 1989).

The only viable option for those without insurance is a self-help group. Narcotics Anonymous and Alcoholics Anonymous are two such self-help organizations. The most common treatment model for both residential and self-help groups is a "Twelve-step approach." This approach, developed by "Bill W." of Alcoholic Anonymous, begins with the admission by the person that he or she is in fact dependent on some chemical substance. The "client" moves through a series of steps designed to increase the level of personal responsibility. The twelfth step is helping someone else with a dependency problem. The therapeutic power of helping someone else is well documented (Reissman, 1963). This treatment model works for approximately a quarter of those who participate. There is an unknown percentage of chronic substance abusers who stop on their own. There are those who would claim that this willpower to quit using the addictive substance without any outside help contradicts the disease theory. Those of you who work in substance abuse treatment will most likely be involved in programs embracing the disease model using knowledge and spirituality as the treatment methods. A few of you may work in programs treating substance abuse with behavioral therapy designed on an individual case-by-case basis and focused on extinguishing behaviors that are dangerous to the client and others.

The behavioral therapy model will become more common as the field of substance abuse treatment moves from being dominated by those who are recovering substance-dependent persons to greater influence from more traditionally trained professionals. An increasing percentage of treatment staff will not only have personal experiences with substance abuse but will also have received professional training. Such fellow staff members are less likely to be dogmatic in their diagnosis and treatment preferences. They will be less likely to label and categorize the substance abusing persons into one large group. More likely, they will see clients as individuals with varying degrees of abuse and dependence and coming from a wide variety of backgrounds. The profile of the helpless and depressed person may not lead such professionals to conclude that the depression was caused by substance abuse. Such professionals may view the patient as having one or more underlying psychological problems, or perhaps a personality disorder. The use of alcohol and other drugs may be symptomatic rather than causative. Such a viewpoint will not be the dominant one in programs where most beginning human-service workers are employed. As this view begins to have more of an impact on treatment programs, we are likely to see a shift from the typical twenty-eight day in-patient treatment programs based on the "Twelve-step" model of the early 1990s. This client population will continue to be an unsettled and rather migrant group who, in addition to their substance abuse, display transient behaviors in terms of family stability, career permanence, and life goals.

Temporary Homes

Families move on the average of once every four years. This rate will increase. People are on the move. Addresses will become more temporary. Even now, we are referred to as occupant or resident by bulk-mail advertisers. The security of a home is being replaced by appliances, furniture, and household gadgets that can be moved from address to address. More children are being cared for by nonrelatives, because parents don't live near the rest of the family. Even children's toys are temporary, with their nonreplaceable plastic parts.

Nostalgia is a reflection of our longing for the way things used to be. Some people try to recapture the security of the past by collecting, using, and even wearing relics and other symbols of past eras, but their security is only symbolic.

As people move through temporary relationships, predictable social games become especially important. These games, ranging from simple rituals to complex life games, are poor substitutes for deep human relationships. Since social games are predictable, they provide some continuity as people move from place to place; however, even the most skillful game-players sense the meaninglessness as they move from one encounter to the next.

As transients, we will be constantly uprooted from our psychological support systems such as the corner bar, the bridge club, the apartment swimming pool, or the lunchtime gang. As we leave each place, we intend to keep in touch, but we won't. We will move on and try to find substitutes for what we have left behind. Others will take our place; we will take somebody else's place. People who "fit" are interchangeable, much like the parts in Eli Whitney's mass-produced Civil War rifles. These trends, which Alvin Toffler (1970) labeled *future shock* and Erikson (1977) defined as a "chronic disaster," threaten the satisfaction of our need to belong. Naisbitt (1984) views such changes as opportunities for those who see a larger picture. Two of the megatrends identified by Naisbitt are the move from centralization toward smaller units and from institutional help toward self help. The problem of homelessness presents one example of these two trends.

Homelessness

Even though there are growing numbers of homeless persons, national-level concern has been minimal. Local efforts and some better known private organizations such as Habitat for Humanity have accepted the challenge rather than federal or state governments.

The number of homeless individuals in the United States has fluctuated during our history. After the Great Depression of the

1930s, the homeless were fewer in number and characterized mostly as chronic alcoholic males (Bahr, 1973; U.S. Department of Housing and Urban Development, 1984; Hock and Slayton, 1989). In recent years, additional homeless subgroups can be characterized (Hopper and Hamberg, 1986; Stefl, 1987; Institute of Medicine, 1988). The homeless mentally ill were discussed in Chapter 5. The prevalence of severe mental disorders, and alcohol and other drug abuse is much higher among the homeless than the general population (Koegel, Burnam, and Farr, 1988). Breakey et al., (1989) have documented increased prevalence of severe physical illness in homeless adults. A history of childhood sexual and/or physical abuse has been found repeatedly across samples of homeless women. Runaway, homeless adolescents present a high level of physical and sexual abuse (Schinn, Knickman, and Weitzman, 1991).

Staff members working in programs for the homeless will be faced with a combination of providing direct services to clients, as well as the challenge of developing community support to provide services to this population. One fact of the homeless phenomenon is that they are effectively disenfranchised. They don't vote, don't have a lobby, and don't make political contributions.

Estimates of the total count of homeless people in the United States have produced divergent and contentious figures ranging from 250,000 (U.S. Department of Housing and Urban Development, 1984) to 550,000 (Burt and Cohen, 1989a) to 3,000,000 homeless individuals (Hombs and Snyder, 1982). Regardless of which figure is more accurate, the numbers continue to grow. As the competition for affordable housing increases, and the discrepancy between the "haves" and the "have-nots" gets larger, homelessness will become an even more pressing issue for human-service providers. Those of you who work in this field will have the challenge of increasing public and political awareness to the point where homelessness as a social issue can compete with issues having more current appeal.

Public Toward Private

Many large, bureaucratic, publicly supported organizations are shrinking in size. Privatization in the form of contracting with private agencies for human services will continue at an accelerated pace. Services formerly run directly by the state and federal governments will become increasingly more private. Federal prisoners will be housed in private jails and other correctional facilities at an increasing rate. Private security agencies will become an even larger industry, replacing some parts of publicly funded police activities.

The provision of foster care services by governmental agencies will continue to be shifted towards private social service organizations. The movement toward educational options that provide parents with alternatives to public education will exacerbate the problems associated with urban public education. This decentralization of social services will not limit the deinstitutionalization of mental patients but will extend and expand throughout the human-services arena. One result will be a relatively small group of private social-service agencies dominating and perhaps controlling the market for the provision of such services.

State and national professional associations will become dominated by the executives and other senior staff members of these private social-service organizations, which will have powerful lobbies at both the state and national levels. Competition will be reduced by the dominance of large subcontractors in this relatively new sector of private enterprise—providing human services to those clients previously served directly by government-run organizations.

Local Community Control

One other major consequence of this governmental decentralization or downsizing will be the rediscovery that local communities are more likely to know what is good for them. This realization will produce mechanisms for more local control, direction, and influence of tax supported human-service programs. This community-based direction will work in cooperation with and under the watchful eye of a professional civil service staff member. These jobs, which require working in communities but also being a state or national employee, will require a set of skills and talents not usually found in traditionally trained college graduates. To maintain a delicate balance between locally empowered voluntary organizations and the statutory requirements will be a demanding management position.

Legal Influences and Special Interests

One of the motivations for the shift from centralized governmental control of direct human services has been the intervention of the courts. In the mid-1970s, federal courts began to direct some correctional institutions in the United States. Issues of overcrowding, humane treatment, and rehabilitation programs have all come under scrutiny. More recently, several states have been successfully sued to provide better social services to client populations. Some courts have gone as far as directing state legislatures to increase select departmental budgets and then to negotiate with those departments for the development and provision of more effective services. One group of adult inmates was successful in a lawsuit requiring the state to provide equal training programs for females. Thus that state was forced by the courts to implement an array of new programs in the face of budget cuts in existing programs. This trend toward treating human problems with legal solutions will be accelerated. As tax-supported governmental agencies move toward the subcontracting model previously discussed, they may insulate themselves legally from malpractice. One of the consequences of this will be to have staff attorneys to protect clients' rights.

Planning and coordination will continue to be short-term and in response to some crisis. One consequence of a democratic electoral process is the inability to do long-term planning for tax-supported programs. National and state budgets are produced by legislatures elected for limited terms, and therefore are adopted for a limited number of fiscal years. The move toward increasing use of profit-making subcontractors for social service, medical care, and education may mediate this effect of short-term management. Such agencies typically will have budgets supported by a mixed funding base which will include tax dollars, philanthropic donations, and support from one or more organized religious groups.

Consumer demand is beginning to have a real impact on human services. The melting-pot concept is being shattered, as groups assert their distinctive interests within the context of racial, ethnic, class, and sexual identities (Isaacs, 1975). Each group wants culturally compatible staff in human-service organizations. Their demands are supported by the differences that exist between groups in life-styles, values, emotional expressiveness, communication patterns, and family structures.

Pressures to amend civil rights legislation will continue to increase as specific minority groups gain recognition and power. Pressure for affirmative action, hiring quotas, and equal representation of professional and nonprofessional staff in tax-supported organizations will increase. Ethnic minorities, gay and lesbian groups, and the handicapped are a few of the minorities which will continue to press for such equal participation.

The Labor Market

There was a time when people dedicated their lives to the organization for which they worked. The company took precedence over everything else. In return for this complete and total dedication, employees received job security, pay raises, promotions, and nice retirement packages (Bennett, 1990). This psychological contract provided security and predictability. Opportunities for advancement and the paths to obtain them were clear cut (Sanderson and Schein, 1986).

Such a culture no longer exists. In the decade of 1980-1990, Fortune 500 companies laid off more than three million people (Tomasko, 1990). As the economy continues to decline and tax dollars decrease, the effect on human-service organizations will be similar to that which is occurring in the corporate world. As retirements occur, these positions are remaining unfilled. Local programs supported by state budgets are being reduced. The "frills" in public schools are being eliminated. Juvenile probation staffs are being cut and those probation officers with seniority are returning to less desirable shift-work jobs in juvenile detention facilities. These are but two examples of a trend in the human-services labor market which new graduates will be facing.

The general labor force will be affected by three significant trends. The skills of the available workers will not match job requirements. Women, minorities, and immigrants will continue occupying a larger share of the work force. Skilled labor shortages will spread throughout all levels of organizations (Hay Group, 1989). This mismatch between employer job requirements and workers' skills will occur at the same time as both corporate and public organizations reduce the numbers in the work force.

The composition of the work force will change. In 1950, the average age of an employee was less than thirty, and 70 percent of these were white males. By the year 2000, one out of every five new labor force entrants will be a minority youth, and the average age of the work force will rise to thirty-nine, and women will constitute 60 percent of the work force.

One of the major emerging issues for the human-service organizations is that approximately 40 percent of the work force is functionally or marginally illiterate. Some 15 percent of the adult population (Brizius and Foster, 1987) fits this category. Our schools are producing graduates who are functionally illiterate at a time when ordinary factory jobs require a high degree of skill. Remediation for this adult population will continue to be one of the most dramatic unmet needs. The absence of such basic skills as reading and writing will further compound the social, political, and economic problems that are associated with the increasing percentages of children and families living in poverty.

In the near future, in an attempt to integrate services, we will see "shopping centers" of health, welfare, and educational services, where clients purchase service with a voucher. Agencies will cash in the vouchers they have collected for the next budget. Those that provide the best services to clients—as judged by the number of client vouchers collected—will be granted the largest budget. The movement has already begun in state colleges and universities. Budgets are often based on credit-hour production—how many students enroll, and how many classes they pass.

Helping, in its various forms, is becoming less professional. There are at least two reasons for this. First, colleges and universities, where most of the helpers are trained, have lowered traditional academic standards in their competition for students. Second, the skills and competencies that are needed in human services are only slightly related to education as we now know it.

"Primary prevention" is becoming a popular phrase. Stop the problems upstream with little dams, so that we don't get a flood in the courts and hospitals. In our primary-prevention work, we have begun (and will continue) to expand programs such as foster-parent training, street therapy, community prevention of mental illness, early-age tutoring, preschool training for handicapped children, and training for infant stimulators. All such programs require staff people who have much more than a formal education.

The effective helpers of tomorrow—including administrators—will need to be recruited and hired on the basis of something more relevant than looks, degrees, and grades. "It will take an unusual human being to develop real rapport with a girl who has had 61 previous placements" (Chicago Bar Association Hearings, 1991). Compared with those who now work in the typical bureaucratic organization, effective staff members of the future will need to be more creative, spontaneous, independent, and self-directed. Traditionally, schools have not encouraged the development of these traits in their students.

Forecasting and preparing for the future costs money. If your organization can barely support its basic services to clients, don't expect much planning. Maybe you will be the one who assumes leadership and changes this situation. In the meantime, enjoy the good feeling you get from a student's achievement, a parolee's job, a runaway's telephone call, an inmate's early release, or a patient's health. After all, you had something to do with it.

Summary

Don't lose your keys. The organization has loaned you metallic keys that open locks; it creates quite a problem if you lose them. The keys to your mental health are even more important. Many people occasionally experience feelings of failure. Help givers usually are poor help takers.

References

Bahr, H. M. 1973. *Skid Row: An Introduction to Disaffiliation.* New York: Oxford University Press.

Bennett, A. 1990. *The Death of the Organization Man.* New York: William Morrow.

Breakey, W. R., Fisher, P. J., Kramer, M., Nestadt, G., Romanoski, A. J., Ross, A., Royall, R. M., and Stine, O. C. 1989. Health and mental health problems of homeless men and women in Baltimore. *Journal of the American Medical Association,* 262, 1352-57.

Brizius and Foster. 1987. *1986 State Policy Data Book.* Alexandria, VA: State Policy Research, Inc.

Burt, M. R., and Cohen, B. E. 1989. *America's Homeless: Numbers, Characteristics, and the Programs That Serve Them.* Washington, D.C.: Urban Institute.

Chicago Bar Association Hearings. 1991. Chicago, IL.

Erikson, E. 1976-77. Living in a world without stable points of reference. *World Issues,* Center for the Study of Democratic Institutions, December/January, 13-14.

Fingarette, H. 1988. *Heavy Drinking.* Berkeley: University of California Press.

Gibbs, N. 1990. Shameful bequests to the next generation. *Time,* October 8, 43.

Gutek, B. A. 1985. *Sex and the Workplace.* San Francisco, CA: Jossey-Bass.

Hay Group. 1989. Linking New Employee Attitudes and Values to Improved Productivity, Cost and Quality: Attracting, Developing and Retaining Employees in the Shifting Labor and Management Market of the 90's.

Hock, C., and Slayton, R. A. 1989. *New Homeless and Old: Community and the Skid Row Hotel.* Philadelphia, PA: Temple University Press.

Hombs, M. E., and Snyder, M. 1982. *Homelessness in America: A Forced March to Nowhere.* Washington, DC: Community for Creative Nonviolence.

Hopper, K., and Hamberg, J. 1986. The Making of America's Homeless: From Skid Row to New Poor. In R. Bratt, C. Hartmann, and A. Meyerson (eds.), *Critical Perspectives on Housing.* Philadelphia, PA: Temple University Press.

Isaacs, H. 1975. *Idols of the Tribe: Group Identity and Political Change.* New York: Harper & Row.

Institute of Medicine. 1988. *Homelessness, Health, and Human Needs.* Washington, DC: National Academy Press.

Koegel, P., Burnam, M. A., and Farr, R. K. 1988. The prevalence of specific psychiatric disorders among homeless individuals in the inner city of Los Angeles. *Archives of General Psychiatry,* 45, 1085-92.

Kolstoe, O. 1975. *College Professoring: or Through Academia with Gun and Camera.* Carbondale and Edwardsville: Southern Illinois University Press.

Krauthammer, C. 1992. In praise of mass hypocrisy. *Time*, April 27, 74.

Manning, P. K. 1972. Locks and Keys: An Essay on Privacy. In J. M. Henslin (ed.), *Down to Earth Sociology*. New York: Free Press.

Naisbitt, J. 1984. *Megatrends*. New York: Warner Books, Inc.

Peele, S. 1989. *Diseasing of America: Addiction Treatment Out of Control*. Library of Congress.

Reissman, F. 1963. *The Helper Therapy Principle*. New York: Basic Books.

Sanderson, S., and Schein, L. 1986. Sizing up the down-sizing era. *Across the Board*, November.

Schinn, M., Knickman, J. R., and Weitzman, B. C. 1991. Social relationships and vulnerability to becoming homeless among poor families. *American Psychologist*, 46, 1180-87.

Stefl, M. 1987. The New Homeless: A National Perspective. In R. D. Bingham, R. E. Green, and S. B. White (eds.), *The Homeless in Contemporary Society*. Newbury Park, CA: Sage.

Thomann, D. A., Strickland, D. E., and Gibbons, J. L., 1989. An Organizational Development Approach to Preventing Sexual Harassment. *College and University Personnel Association Journal*, December, 40(3), 34-43.

Toffler, A. 1970. *Future Shock*. New York: Random House.

Tomasko, R. 1990. *Downsizing: Reshaping the Corporation for the Future*. New York: Amacom.

U.S. Department of Housing and Urban Development. 1984. *A Report to the Secretary on the Homeless and Emergency Shelters*. Washington, DC: U.S. Department of Housing and Urban Development.

Weston, D. R., Ivins, B., Zuckerman, B., Jones, C., and Lopez, R. 1989. *Drug Exposed Babies: Research and Clinical Issues, Zero to Three*. National Center for Clinical Infant Programs 9(5), 5, June.

White, J. G., Lehmann, L. C., Ragone, L. M., Buonocore, I., and Hansford, C. R. 1990. *Crack Babies*. Office of Inspector General (HHS), OEI-03-89-01540, June.

Index

Acceptable work rate, 7
Accountability, 31, 36, 48, 109
Accrediting, 3, 156
Accrediting bodies, 3
Actors, 9, 20
Adjustment
  to change, 147, 148
  to failure, 13
  forms of, 61
  patterns of, 57, 81
  of teachers, 74
Administrative approval, 135
Adult reading teachers, 96
Advertising, 2, 46
Affirmative action, 4, 171
Agency administrators, 36
Aiding, 1
AIDS
  epidemic, 121
  HIV positive newborns, 95
  people with, 80, 83, 121
  spread of, 143
  tattoo for, 121
Alcoholics Anonymous, 166
Alcoholism, 153, 166
Allocation, 44, 72
Alpert, J. L., 146, 153
Alutto, J. A., 74, 75, 82
Amateur professionals, 59, 60
Antabuse, 166
Appelbaum, P. S., 86-88, 99
Application materials, 3
Applications, 1, 3, 44
Ashcroft, J., 109, 111
Assistants, 44, 53, 96
At-risk population, 150
Authority
  appeal to higher, 129
  California Youth Authority, 87

figures, 18, 53
necessity of, 110
normal lines of, 159
over clients, 47
relationship to control, 47
in relationships, 40
testing of, 11

Bachrach, L. L., 87, 88, 99
Baer, B. L., 126, 139
Bahr, H. M., 169, 174
Baldridge, J. V., 58, 82, 128, 132, 139
Bargain, 8
Behavioral therapy model, 167
Bennett, A., 68, 172, 174
Berliner, A., 41, 53
Bernstein, G. S., 14, 15, 34
Bill W., 166
Billingsley, A., 60, 82
Blake, R. R., 40, 53
Blau, P. M., 60, 82
Board and care, 91, 92, 96
Board of directors, 36, 98, 99
Bowles, S., 73, 82
Bradby, M., 75, 82
Braswell, M., 19, 34
Breakey, W. R., 169, 174
Brizius, 172, 174
Brown, L., 76, 82
Buckley, W. F., Jr., 121, 139
Bureaucracy
  as a complex environment, 124, 125
  as means of organizing, 35
  in organizations, 12, 41, 72, 86, 110
  professionals in, 98, 132
  as rule-following, 71
Bureaucratic celebrations, 160
Burned out, 23, 118, 120
Burnout, 117-122, 139

Burt, M. R., 169, 174

California Youth Authority, 87
Case workers, 96
Chamberlin, L. J., 107, 111
Change strategy, 133, 134
Chicago Bar Association, 173, 174
Child abuse, 150, 164, 165
Chronic disaster, 168
Civilian Conservation Corps, 142
Clary, E. G., 80, 82
Clients
  abuse 26, 27, 114, 169
  attempt to psych you out, 21, 162
  dealing with, 9-12, 20, 21
  expectations regarding, 5, 17, 18, 21
  history, 6, 18, 20, 22, 33, 70, 104
  as important people, 1, 13-15, 30-32
  as more experienced, 19, 60, 162
  power, 16, 17, 31, 47, 58, 59
  as powerless, 102, 103, 106, 160
  relationship to volunteers, 77-81
  as a resource, 37, 57, 72, 104, 109
  rights of, 30, 31, 67, 167, 170, 171
  as staff members, 32, 55
  view of you, 23, 119, 163
  as volunteers, 116, 134
Colonial America, 85
Committees, 99, 155, 156
Community-based programs, 85
Community Mental Health Centers Act
  of, 1963 88
Community Referral Services, 3
Community residential care, 88, 91, 92
Community support program, 94
Compete, 8, 44, 103, 109, 111, 126, 147,
  169
Conflict, 44, 61, 72, 78, 138
  acceptance of, 58, 136, 147
  between professionals, 106, 108, 117,
    133
  in humor, 46
  management, 40
  in meetings and the system, 62, 103,
    104, 122, 137, 143
  opportunity for change, 8, 9, 46, 57,
    136
  resolution, 9, 10, 60, 61, 128, 146
  stress, 4, 107, 136
  with rules and norms, 7, 8, 10, 57, 60
Conformists, 61
Consultants, 155, 156
Consumer demand, 171
Consumerism, 30
Content of staff meetings, 62

Control, 44, 50, 55, 58, 70, 71, 135, 138
  birth, 143
  of clients, 21, 48, 59, 78
  as an end, 47, 85, 117, 133, 137
  forms of, 71
  government, 86, 99
  local, 36, 170
  loss of, 121, 122
  organizational, 40, 46-48, 52, 69, 103,
    127, 128
  over programs, 79
Conway, J. A., 42, 53, 59, 82
Corporate-sponsored child care, 32
Counseling, 1, 121, 163
  with clients, 21, 48, 59, 78
  genetic, 144
  paraprofessional, 68, 104
  premarital, 148
  rehabilitation, 65
  by supervisors, 117
Counselors, 1, 3, 32, 49, 70, 80, 83, 145
Court administrators' offices, 3
Cover letter, 3, 4
Coworkers, 55, 57, 59, 81, 157, 160
  attitudes of, 5, 13, 21, 58, 63, 120, 121
  behavior of, 8, 50, 118, 135, 161
  support from, 9-11, 17, 51, 122, 123

Data processing system, 3
Decentralization, 170
Deinstitutionalization movement, 86,
  91
Delinquent youth, 80
Department of Health and Human
  Services, 102, 111, 112, 153
Devito, R. A., 128, 139
Domalewski, R. M., 76, 82
Domestic social problems, 164
Driver, D. E., 77, 82
Drucker, P. F., 36, 53
Drug abuse, 95, 144, 146, 165, 166, 169
Dutch uncle talk, 12

Eclectic approach, 127
Edelwich, J., 117, 139
Edgar, D. E., 74, 82
Educating, 1, 126, 139, 140
Efficiency, 36, 48, 56, 98
Erikson, E., 168, 174
Established professionals, 59, 60
Etzioni, A., 40, 44, 54, 83
Evaluation, 32, 38, 39, 43, 51, 55, 72,
  110, 152, 156
Experiential learning techniques, 151
Expressive, 40, 41, 44

Extension class, 157

Failure, 13, 77, 86, 89, 131, 145, 146, 150, 162, 163, 174
Family care homes, 91, 92
Family preservation programs, 165
Feedback, 11, 12, 121
Felner, R. D., 149, 152, 153
Fielding, N. G., 76, 82
Fingarette, H., 166, 174
Fish, 75
Fletcher, J., 19, 34, 82
Focus groups, 31
Food stamps, 96
Fourteen Ounces of Prevention, 145, 154
Francis, R. G., 72, 82
French, W. L., 127, 139
Friedlander, F., 57, 82
Friedman, D. E., 32, 34
Furst, L. G., 47, 54
Fustaro, S., 92, 93, 99
Future shock, 15, 34, 168, 175

Gamsen, Z. F., 138, 139
General Assistance, 96, 142
Geriatric mental patients, 47, 80, 134
Gibbs, N., 145, 149, 152, 153, 164, 174
Gig, 77
Goffman, E., 56, 70, 83, 104, 111
Golden, O., 13, 36, 54, 127, 139
Great Depression, 86, 98, 142, 169
Green, A. D., 72, 83
Green peas, 75
Guiding, 1, 157
Gutek, B. A., 159, 174

Haller, E. J., 74, 83
Hay Group, 172, 174
Hayner, N. S., 11, 14
Hegar, R. L., 36, 54
Helper therapy principle, 80, 175
Helping institutions, 1, 107
Hemming, H., 95, 99
Henslin, J. M., 65, 83, 175
Hersey, P., 40, 43, 54
High-commitment, 75
High-level sponsorship, 109
Hiring, 3, 4, 35, 55, 104, 155, 171
HIV. *see* AIDS
Hock, C., 169, 174
Hodgkinson, H., 146, 153
Hoffer, E., 6, 14, 55, 83
Hombs, M. E., 169, 174
Homelessness, 77, 92, 93, 168, 169, 174, 175

Hooker, C. P., 51, 54
Hopper, K., 169, 174
Hospitality rooms, 158
Human Service System, 102
Humanistic, 13
Humor, 12, 46, 123

Immediate supervisor, 21, 45, 128, 129, 133
In-service training, 52, 157
Incest, 165
Influence flow, 50, 51
Informal control, 71
Informal power, 44
Informal shadow organization, 52, 75
Information chain, 2
Innovation by "groping along," 127
Inspecting, 156
Institute of Medicine, 169, 175
Institutional control, 71
Institutional-training process, 70
Instrumental, 40, 44
Interagency partnerships, 108, 111, 139
Interdependence, 9
Internship, 13
Interview, 1, 4, 5, 13, 56, 157
Isaacs, H., 171, 17
Isolation, 9, 25, 77, 127, 136

Jacobs, J. B., 18, 19, 34, 46, 54, 75, 83
Job, 5, 7, 33, 34, 39, 69, 75, 77, 93
    applications, 3-5, 56
    description, 51-53, 60, 70, 81, 122, 149, 153, 165, 172
    environment, 13, 26, 45, 59, 61, 118
    expectations, 15, 21, 32, 38, 45, 101, 113
    for clients, 67, 72, 108, 131, 173
    Job Corp, 142
    performance, 57, 124, 164
    related anxiety, 9, 11, 14, 20, 25, 42, 53, 118, 120, 123
    selection/interview, 1, 2, 13, 78
    socialization, 76, 81, 117, 119, 121, 126
    supervisors, 43, 44, 46, 99, 125
Job-related sex, 158, 159
Jourard, S., 15, 34

Kahn, R. L. 136, 139
Kennedy, J. F., 88
Kidwell, K. D., 102, 109, 111
Koegel, P., 169, 175
Kolstoe, O., 156, 175
Kramer, P., 60, 75, 83, 146, 153, 174
Krauthammer, C., 158, 175

Labor market, 172
Landesmann-Dwyer, S., 95, 100
Lawler, E. E., III, 4, 14, 57, 83
Lawyers, 36, 105
Lefton, M., 104, 111
Legal aid, 105, 106
Legal influences, 170
Levy, L., 127, 139
Lewis, D., 88, 89, 100
Licata, J. W., 11, 16, 34
Licensing bureaus, 3
Limited sociogram, 9
Linkages, 102, 108, 128
Local community control, 170
Locks and keys, 163, 175
Lofquist, W. A., 150, 153
Lortie, D. C., 73-75, 83

MacGregor, D., 40, 54
Mandell, B. R., 36, 54, 88, 100, 120, 139
Manning, P. K., 163, 175
Marcus, P. M., 48, 54
Marso, R. N., 74, 83
Maslach, C., 120, 122, 123, 139
Maslow, A. H., 15, 34
Massachusetts, 31, 73, 87
Maxwell, A. D., 37, 54
May, R., 15, 34
McArthur, J., 74, 83
Mediate, 8, 171
Medical prevention, 148
Medicheck, 114
Melaville, A. I., 109, 111, 128, 139
Menges, R. J., 56, 83
Mental health, 95, 103, 104
   agency, 28, 95, 105, 106
   centers, 18, 90, 144
   deinstitutionalization in, 87, 98
   federal involvement in, 86, 88
   of homeless persons, 93
   institutions, 89
   jobs in, 3, 99
   maintaining your own, 14, 72, 164,
      174
   of supervisors, 117
   technicians, 96
Mental Health Study Act of 1955, 87
Mentally ill, 29, 85-96, 98, 100, 154,
   169
Merit judgments, 51
Millham, S., 71, 83
Milofsky, C., 98, 100
Moore, R. H., 80, 83
Morganthau, T., 92, 94, 100
Morris, D., 80, 83

Morrow-Howell, N., 81, 84
Mueller, D. P., 143, 150, 153

N.I.M.B.Y., 95
Naisbitt, J., 168, 175
Narcotics Anonymous, 166
National Commission on Children, 102,
   109, 111, 143, 153
National Institute on Alcohol Abuse
   and Alcoholism, 153
Neglect, 92, 120, 146, 150
Nelson, D. L., 70, 84
New staff members, 1, 16, 22, 55, 56
No rat rule, 76, 77
Nonexchange, 36
Nonprofessional, 64, 67, 171
Norms, 63, 70
   as barter, 11
   as control, 48, 50, 71
   defined, 6
   employee's problems with, 7, 10, 26
   in the organization, 52, 55, 62, 75, 76,
      79, 136, 159, 161
   in outreach programs, 94
Nurses, 1, 11, 17, 69, 75, 96, 123
   charge, 45, 114
   levels of commitment, 75
   new, 60
   patterns of job advancement, 74
   socialization of, 74
   student, 6, 137
Nursing, 1, 65, 75, 121
   care plans, 156
   performance, 11, 67
   supervisor, 12, 41, 47, 69
Nursing homes, 35, 88, 90, 91, 96, 107,
   148

O'Banion, T., 15, 34
Occupational therapists, 96
Office of Inspector General, 102, 111,
   112, 165, 175
Open hiring, 3
Organizational change, 40, 124, 126,
   127
Organizational continuity, 98
Organizational control, 47, 52
Organizational reorganization, 48
Orientation, 71, 76, 79, 82, 104, 160
Oskamp, S., 88, 100

Paraprofessional, 64, 65, 134
Parental involvement, 151
Parliamentary procedure, 46
Peele, S., 166, 175
Pepper, B., 152, 154

Personal journal, 20, 33, 138
Personal-support system, 8, 14
Personnel file, 3, 156
Planned questions, 5
Plodders, 57-59
Poor school performance, 150
Potential adverse effects, 151, 152
Power, 19, 36, 40, 46, 47, 61, 74
  of assistants, 44
  of clients, 31
  of employers, 55
  as factor in innovation, 128, 132, 135,
    171
  roots of, 123
  of teachers, 73
  therapeutic, 167
Prevention programs, 141, 144, 145,
  148, 149-154, 165
Price, R. H., 145-148, 152, 154
Prichard, R. D., 57, 84
Priorities, 8, 50, 93, 103
Prison guards, 1, 46, 75, 123
Privacy, 31, 163, 175
Private security agencies, 170
Privatization, 169
Probation, 55, 56, 76, 78, 80, 144
  goals, 104
  juvenile, 78, 109, 172
  officer, 22, 32, 38, 110
Probationary reviews, 56
Professionalism, 58, 97, 100, 109, 110
Program theory, 141, 142, 144, 153
Psychiatric aides, 12, 96, 114
Psychiatric nurses, 96
Psychiatrists, 96
Psychodynamic process, 73
Psychological contract, 2, 172
Psychological support, 9, 161, 168
Psychologists, 1, 15, 66, 78, 96, 109
Public defender, 3

Reality shock, 73-75, 83, 84
Reconcile, 8, 62
Recreational therapists, 96
Recruitment practices, 3
Referral, 3, 102, 106, 107, 111, 157
Reform schools, 30, 104
Reformers, 58
Reissman, F., 167, 175
Resolution, 8, 9, 146
Responsible revolutionaries, 55
Robbins, S. P., 61, 84, 136, 140
Rochefort, D. A., 87-89, 92, 93, 95, 100,
  147, 149, 152, 154
Roney, J., Jr., 51, 54

Rousseau, A. M., 92, 93, 100
Russo, J. R., 48, 54, 63, 70, 80, 84, 135,
  140

Sanctioning colleagues, 74
Sanderson, S., 172, 175
Sarcasm, 12
Satellite housing, 92
Scheier, I. H., 78, 84
Schein, I. H., 70, 84, 172, 175
Schinn, M., 169, 175
School failure, 145, 146, 150
Schorr, L. B., 110, 111, 127, 140, 143,
  154
Schwitzgebel, R. K., 31, 34
Secretaries, 64, 67-69
Security institution, 30, 66
Self-help group, 166
Self-justification, 2
Semiprofessional, 74
Service delivery, 9, 109, 110, 155
Service integration, 99, 102, 109
Serving, 1, 81, 144
Sexual harassment, 155, 159, 160, 175
Shadish, W. R., 88, 89, 100
Shadow organization, 50-53, 75
Sheridan, J. E., 2, 14
Sierra Club, 73
Skilled labor shortages, 172
Smith, L. M., 21, 34, 48, 73, 84, 104, 112
Social security, 86, 93, 96, 101
Social workers, 1, 96, 103, 109
  in juvenile detention centers, 66
  and lawyers, 105
  in schools, 38
  socialization of, 70-72
Social-casework agencies, 30
Socialization, 13, 56, 70-77, 81-84, 118,
  160
Solution, 9, 65, 128, 130, 159
Specialized service-oriented personnel,
  67
Staff meetings, 58, 61-63, 81
Staff recruitment, 55, 56
State Reorganization Commission, 109,
  112
Stefl, M., 169, 175
Structural control, 71
Student brinkmanship, 11, 34
Subordinate/superordinate relation-
  ships, 40
Supervision, 55, 77, 79, 83, 91, 92, 146,
  151
Supervisors, 1, 7, 9, 14, 41, 42, 66, 129,
  131

budget concerns, 72
burnout of, 120, 122
and conflict, 9, 46, 117, 136
immediate, 44-46, 137
as information source, 46
and norms, 52, 55, 56
and reorganization, 49
in shadow organization, 40, 51, 53
socialization of, 74
and staff meetings, 61
and victims, 58
Sympathy, 93, 160, 161

Teachers, 1, 6, 32, 33, 70, 75, 81, 86, 96,
    104, 123, 141, 162
boards and, 38
conflicts and, 61, 107
helplessness of, 116, 117, 119
and norms, 10, 11, 21
and prevention programs, 146, 147,
    149, 160
shadow organization, 51, 68
socialization of, 72-74
and status quo, 56
student, 137, 138
as trainers, 77
training of, 157
Teaching, 1, 42, 61, 69, 74, 75, 116, 121,
    158
burnout, 122
coworkers, 17
and organizational control, 47
student, 68, 73, 137
Teenage pregnancy, 143, 150
Teenage substance abuse, 150
Temporary homes, 168
Tertiary prevention, 144
Thomann, D. A., 159, 175
Toffler, A., 15, 34, 168, 175
Tomasko, R., 172, 175
Torrey, E. F., 89, 94, 95, 100
Trades, 30
Training, 1, 9, 29, 59, 61, 66, 69, 70, 77,
    108, 118, 137, 147, 151, 156, 171,
    173
of administrators, 43

college, 45, 76
in-service, 52, 157
mental health, 86
of new staff members, 55
nurse, 75
parent-effectiveness, 144
pre-service, 74
skill, 30
specialized, 64, 96, 109, 167
teacher, 73
vocational, 130,
of volunteers, 78
Treating, 1, 23, 113, 138, 167, 171
Triple headers, 3
Twelve-step approach, 166

U.S. Department of Housing and Urban
    Development, 169, 175
Unionism, 58
United Way, 3, 36

Veenman, S., 73, 74, 84
Volunteer, 77, 81, 86, 98, 116, 156
boards, 97
effectiveness, 80
movement, 77
problems, 78, 79
profile, 78
tutoring services, 108
Vroom, V. H., 2, 14

Wade, L. L., 133, 140
Wanous, J. P., 2, 14
Ward attendants, 1
Wasserman, H., 58, 72, 84
Web, 9
Wells, K., 149, 152, 154
Weston, D. R., 164, 175
White, J. G., 165, 175
Willower, D. J., 11, 16, 34, 47, 54
Wright, B. D., 73, 84
Women, Infants, and Children, 145
Wubbels, T., 74, 84

Yessian, M. R., 102, 112
Youth supervisors, 1, 66